Thames & Hudson

CHRISTOPHER FITZ-SIMON

the abbey theatre

IRELAND'S NATIONAL THEATRE: THE FIRST 100 YEARS

To John McColgan

First published in paperback in the United States of
America in 2003 by Thames & Hudson Inc.,
500 Fifth Avenue, New York, New York 10110

thamesandhudsonusa.com

Library of Congress Catalog Card Number
2003100804

ISBN 0-500-28426-1

Printed and bound in Singapore by CS Graphics

endpapers
The audience at the popular comedy *A Jew Called
Sammy* by John McCann during the Abbey Theatre's
residence at the Queen's Theatre, Dublin, following
the fire of 1951.

half-title page
The Abbey Theatre colophon designed by Elenore
Monsell in 1904 remains in daily use 100 years later.

frontispiece
Kate Flynn, Donal McCann and John Kavanagh in
Joe Dowling's 1981 production of *Faith Healer* by
Brian Friel, from the poster by Brendan Foreman.
Originally produced on Broadway without success,
this production disclosed a work of immense emotional
and technical subtlety, and is regarded by many
as Friel's masterwork.

opposite
Anita Reeves as Mrs Malaprop in RB Sheridan's
The Rivals in 1998.

ABHANN PRODUCTIONS LTD

• •

contents

It is astonishing to think that in its 100-year history the Abbey Theatre has produced close to 1,000 plays on its two stages. Notwithstanding the fact that this number includes double and even triple bills of one-act plays in the early years, this is an impressive record and forms the backbone of Irish dramatic literature in the twentieth century.

Through its writers, the Abbey was a potent voice for the emerging Irish nation, and the theatre continues today to chart and articulate the profound changes in Irish society at the beginning of the new millennium. Gregory, Synge, O'Casey and Yeats lit a torch which is now passing via Murphy, Friel, Leonard, Kilroy and Keane to the young writers of today: Marina Carr, Sebastian Barry, Jim Nolan, Billy Roche and many others.

The Abbey is justly proud of that unbroken tradition of its great plays and the actors, directors and designers who have animated them. But to earn these great plays the Abbey has had to hold its nerve and keep faith with the unpredictable and precarious journey of its writers throughout their careers. Arguably, keeping that faith was its greatest service and its greatest glory. In the words of Samuel Beckett we 'try again, fail again, fail better'.

Christopher Fitz-Simon, himself a former artistic director and literary manager of the Abbey, has, in this survey of the Abbey century, captured fairly and judiciously in words and in images the glory and the imperfection of the way, and the resilience of the wayfarers.

Ben Barnes
Artistic Director, National Theatre Society,
The Abbey and Peacock Theatres

● ●

The Abbey Theatre play most frequently produced throughout the world is Sean O'Casey's *Juno and the Paycock.* First performed in 1924, the production in 2000 with Catherine Walsh as Juno Boyle and Eanna MacLiam as Johnny Boyle was directed by Ben Barnes and designed by Monica Frawley.

preface

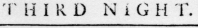

THIRD NIGHT.

This present *Thursday*, being the 9th of *February*, 1758,
Will be presented, a TRAGEDY, called, The

EARL of ESSEX.

Written by *HENRY BROOKE*, Esq;

The Part of ESSEX to be performed by

Mr. SHERIDAN,

Burleigh, Mr. HURST,

Southampton by Mr. DEXTER,

Raleigh, Mr. STORER,

Nottingham by Mrs. KENNEDY,
Rutland by Miss KENNEDY,

And, the Part of Queen Elizabeth to be performed by

Mrs. FITZ-HENRY.

(Being her third Appearance in that Character)

The Characters drest in the Habits of the Times.

To which will be added, (the second Night) a *Pantomime Entertainment,*
called, The

WHIM: Or, *Harlequin Villager.*

With new *Scenes, Musick* and other *Decorations.*
The Character of Harlequin by Mr. KING,
Clown by Mr. SPARKS,
'Squire Gawky by Mr. GLOVER,
Pantaloon *Mr. HAMILTON,*
Drawer *Mr. MESSINK,*
Venus Miss MASON,
Colombine by Mrs. KENNEDY,

With a *NEW DANCE,*

By SIGNOR TIOLI,
Miss BAKER, &c.

the Abbey Theatre, Dublin, opened to the public on 27 December 1904. Its lessees were, and remain, the National Theatre Society Ltd. During its 100 years of production it has presented 742 new plays, many of which are frequently performed in other countries. Among its numerous non-literary distinctions are its apparent indestructibility – no producing management in the English-speaking world has been in continuous operation for so long – and the fact that it was the earliest theatre company in the same international arena to receive annual government subvention.

Drama, in its usual Western meaning, was unknown in early Irish society, which lacked the large urban settlements that provide the theatre audience. With the formal establishment of city corporations and guilds following the Anglo-Norman invasion of 1169, religious drama on Christian themes flourished to some extent, but with nothing like the splendour of language and spectacle for which York, Valenciennes and other centres were famous. Ireland's first conventional theatre on Werburgh Street in Dublin (1637) was an entirely colonial enterprise, for plays and players were drawn from London in order to entertain the English administration and the military garrison at Dublin Castle. The celebrated Theatre Royal (1687) in Smock Alley – a playhouse much frequented by the local bourgeoisie and (after a time) employing local talent – nonetheless took its cue from across the water. Aspiring dramatic authors of Irish birth and education found it necessary to move to the centre of activity, which was London, becoming (whether they thought about it in this way or not) the Irish dramatic diaspora.

The 'colonial' and 'diasporic' strands naturally overlapped. The first was what Ireland took in, like the washing. The second was what Ireland sent out, like smoothed linen. Both strands continued into the twentieth century, when the colonial drained away in a gurgle of murky foam, and the diasporic was absorbed into what might be termed the 'vernacular': that which is associated with the innovations of the Abbey Theatre.

Until the latter part of the twentieth century there was a tendency to separate the diasporic and vernacular strands; commentators outside Ireland found it difficult to accept the existence of a long-standing 'Irish School' which included playwrights such as Farquhar, Goldsmith and Wilde alongside

An eighteenth-century playbill from the Theatre Royal, Smock Alley, Dublin, for a production featuring Thomas Sheridan (1721–88), a distinguished member of the Sheridan dynasty of Irish writers and theatrical entrepreneurs. The bust by Thomas Kirk represents his son, Richard Brinsley Sheridan (1751–1816), author of *The Rivals*, *The School for Scandal* and other plays.

introduction

before the abbey theatre: can there have been such a time in ireland?

O'Casey, Beckett and Friel. When the present author's book *The Irish Theatre* was published in 1983, overseas critical response was generally incredulous on this issue. That outlook has now changed. Significantly, when the leading British theatre director Richard Eyre discussed Ireland's prodigious contribution to Western drama in his millennium television series and its accompanying book *Changing Stages* he did not need to make distinctions: these were all Irish playwrights, wherever they chose to live or whatever society they exposed on the stage.

There is one obvious connector between the diasporic and vernacular modes, and that is George Bernard Shaw. If we look back in time from 1904 to Shaw's London-Irish antecedents and forward to the Abbey Theatre's first century of production, it immediately becomes clear that the Abbey's founders saw the work of exiled Irish playwrights as part of their inheritance – provided it was good enough. Thus, during the Abbey's first twenty-five years, Goldsmith's two major plays were produced, as were one of Sheridan's, one of Wilde's, and eleven by the still very much alive Shaw. It is noteworthy that the founders did not select plays by these authors' English contemporaries – none of whom, it may have been argued, produced work of the same quality.

It is a curious fact that the most enduring comedies in the English language, from Congreve's *Love for Love* in 1695 to Wilde's *The Importance of Being Earnest* in 1895, flowed from the pens of these émigré Irish. Why should this be so? They possessed the edge, and the edginess, of the outsider. They were observers of life's feast in their adopted land. They had the advantage of distance and discovery. They tended to share that sceptical view which is the refuge of the unsettled, the unhappy, the *déraciné*. They had a way of expressing things which was different: as Jorge Luis Borges has suggested, it was sufficient that these (and other) Irish writers working in the English language should have 'felt different'.

Very few critics now recall that there already existed in Ireland a vibrant strand of vernacular theatre at the precise time when Yeats and his collaborators were drawing up their plan of action for what was to become the Abbey Theatre. Indeed, it was partly through the influence of Yeats, Lady Gregory and Edward Martyn that this 'national Irish drama' became sidelined from the stage picture of the Ireland which they were at pains to create. It was a populist theatre. Its plays were usually composed in the melodramatic form, requiring numerous and often spectacular changes of scenery. What distinguished them from their English counterparts was that almost all dealt with patriotic Irish themes: the lovely heroine was here a representation of a pure young Ireland, the dashing hero was fighting for his country's freedom and the dastardly villain was as like as not a usurping English landlord or a scheming redcoat. The chief character was often a revolutionary leader from a previous era – Michael Dwyer, for example, or Robert Emmet – the passage of time removing (it may have been supposed) any offence that might have been given to the authorities at Dublin Castle. Plays peculiar to contemporary issues, where subversive content could not be disguised in period costume, were cloaked in entertaining dialogue.

● ●

The 'national Irish drama' was performed on the stages of the largest theatres in Belfast, Cork and Dublin – most particularly, the Queen's Theatre in Dublin. Many of the plays were presented in metropolitan theatres in Britain and the United States. In Ireland, the recognizable settings, the local references in the script and the homely accents of the players attracted very large attendances. The prototype was the work of the most frequently performed playwright in the English language of the Victorian era, Dublin-born Dion Boucicault. His 'Irish Trilogy' – *The Colleen Bawn* (1860), *Arrah-na-Pogue* (1864) and *The Shaughran* (1874) – became staples of the Kennedy Miller Company at the Queen's Theatre, Dublin, as well as on tour at home and abroad, and gave rise to somewhat similar work by other writers. These plays, with their rousing patriotic sentiments startlingly juxtaposed with rustic drollery, were anathema to Yeats and most of his circle, sensitive as they were to the notion of the nobility of Irish art and culture.

These plays were not necessarily deficient in intellectual and artistic qualities. Hubert O'Grady's *The Gommoch* (1877), *The Eviction* (1880), *Emigration* (1883), *The Famine* (1886) and *The Priest Hunter* (1893) were as critical of society as any reformist theatre director could wish; an attempt by the Castle to ban *The Eviction* was successfully resisted by the management. JW Whitbread's *The Ulster Hero* contains dialogue as pithy as that of Shaw, and its nationalist stance was distinctly controversial when the play was produced at the Theatre Royal, Belfast, in 1903. Yeats, musing some thirty years later upon the possibility that his and Gregory's *Cathleen ní Houlihan* (1902) may have 'sent out/ Certain men the English shot', clearly had no idea that the patriotic dramas staged contemporaneously in the larger theatres probably 'sent out' far more men, if only because the audiences were much more numerous.

It is tempting to surmise that when Whitbread produced his new historical drama *Sarsfield* at the Queen's on 26 December 1904 he was hoping to snatch attention from the Abbey's opening performance, announced for the following night. In the event, *Sarsfield* received generally favourable notices, while those that covered Yeats' highly concentrated poetic drama *On Baile's Strand* and Lady Gregory's charming rustic comedy *Spreading the News* were nothing if not mixed. It is more likely, however, that the Queen's gave little attention to the appearance of a small theatre which appeared to be the brainchild of yet another group of impractical visionaries, and which would fade away once its perpetrators had moved on to some other arcane pastime.

The opposite happened. The popular patriotic melodramas vanished with the advent of the motion picture and the achievement of Irish independence. Yeats and his followers remained true to the 'high ambition' expressed in their resoundingly phrased manifesto of 1898. Their idealism, their sense of national purpose, their literary precocity and their determination to succeed in spite of unmannerly taunts from, it seemed, all quarters, resulted in the creation of a theatre which, within a very few years, would become the admiration and envy of the Western world.

top
Sir Godfrey Kneller's portrait of
William Congreve (1670–1728) in the
National Gallery of Ireland. Congreve's
most enduring plays are *Love for Love*
and *The Way of the World*.

above left
Triple portrait by Nicholas Crowley
showing the popular Irish actor-manager-
playwright Tyrone Power as Conor
O'Gorman in *The Groves of Blarney* by
Anna Maria Fielding (1797–1841), now
in the Collection of the Tyrone Guthrie
Centre at Annaghmakerrig.

Peg Woffington (1714–60) was the
leading Irish actress of her century. She
declared that Sir Harry Wildair in the
Irish playwright George Farquhar's *The
Constant Couple* that 'half London thinks
I am a man!' James Quin replied: 'The
other half knows you to be a woman!'

The statue of Oliver Goldsmith
(1728–74) by Foley stands outside
Trinity College, Dublin. *She Stoops to
Conquer* was the most performed
comedy in the English language for
over 100 years after his death, and is
still in the international repertoire.

Bryan's caricature of Dionysius Lardner
Boucicault (1820–90), the most widely
performed English-language playwright
in the Victorian era. His 'Irish Trilogy' –
The Colleen Bawn, Arrah-na-Pogue and
The Shaughran – was anathema to the
founders of the Irish Literary Theatre.

Poster by Beardsley for plays by two Irish authors in 1894. John Todhunter (1839–1916) was an active member of the Irish Literary Society in London; his plays are now deservedly forgotten. William Butler Yeats (1865–1939) went on to become the most important poet to write in the English language over the next half-century and was the inspirational force behind the Irish dramatic movement.

Patriotic melodramas by Fagan, Fitzgerald, O'Grady, Whitbread and others were enjoyed by huge audiences in metropolitan theatres at the time of the foundation of the National Theatre Society, continuing well into the twentieth century. Whitbread's *Sarsfield* was first produced in 1904 at the Queen's Theatre, Dublin, on the night prior to the opening of the Abbey Theatre.

Polychrome statue of Oscar Wilde
(1854–1900) by Danny Osborne in
Merrion Square, Dublin, opposite the
house where the author of *Salomé*
and *The Importance of Being Earnest*
grew up. Wilde's descent into illness
and death removed from the Irish
dramatic movement the possibility of
an extraordinary collaboration.

Drawing by Raymond McGrath of
the interior of the Abbey Theatre
as it appeared from 1904 up to the
fire of 1950. Originally the Mechanics'
Theatre, it was renovated for the
National Theatre Society by the
architect Joseph Holloway, Annie
Horniman having provided the funds.

having been sparsely though adequately refurbished for the National Theatre Society through the munificence of the English tea heiress AEF Horniman, the almost derelict Mechanics' Theatre at the intersection of Abbey and Marlborough streets in Dublin reopened in 1904 as the Abbey Theatre. Its programme emerged as the culmination of seven years of activity that began at one of those chance meetings where latent thoughts take fire as like minds interact. The rainswept home of the eccentric Count de Basterot overlooking Galway Bay provided the setting for afternoon tea when the intense young poet William Butler Yeats, the philanthropic landowner Edward Martyn and his neighbour Augusta Isabella, ebullient widow of the colonial administrator Sir William Gregory of Coole Park, found themselves discussing the need for a theatre in Dublin. This theatre would 'express the deeper thoughts and emotions of Ireland'.

This now mythic tea party in the summer of 1897 resulted in the formation of the Irish Literary Theatre. The 1890s was a comparatively calm and prosperous period, following the decades of famine, agrarian disturbance and organized rebellion. There was a real temptation to consider an Ireland inspired by the notion of a Celtic Golden Age, the existence of which seemed to become more tangible through the work of archivists,

archaeologists and linguists, not to mention politicians, poets and writers of fiction. The 1890s saw the formation of a number of nationally disposed associations – the Gaelic League, the Irish Race Convention, the Trades Union Conference, the annual Oireachtas cultural festival and the Feiseanna Cheoil (competitions in music, dance and verse-speaking). The prospect of Home Rule seemed less remote. Yet, as far as the professional theatre was concerned, almost everything was imported, from Brandon Thomas' *Charley's Aunt* to Mrs Patrick Campbell in Maeterlinck's *Pelléas and Mélisande*, from the Moody Manners Opera Company singing in Italian to Sarah Bernhardt playing in French. Only the 'patriotic plays' at the Queen's Theatre were home-produced, and they were dismissed by the founders of the Irish Literary Theatre as 'buffoonery'.

The earliest Irish Literary Theatre productions – Yeats' imagistic verse drama *The Countess Cathleen* and Martyn's ponderous Ibsenite *The Heather Field* – were presented successfully in spite of a religious controversy regarding the alleged 'souls for sale' element in the former, at the Antient Concert Rooms in Dublin in May 1899. Both plays were cast with London actors recommended by the intrusively helpful novelist and social observer George Moore. The Irish actor WG (Willie) Fay, immensely taken with the group's concept

• •

remote, spiritual and ideal

of playwriting, found the casting quite ludicrous. His brother Frank agreed that if there was to be a modern Irish drama 'it must be played by Irish actors, for English actors could never get the atmosphere right'. The Fays, much influenced by André Antoine's Théâtre Libre, ran a semi-professional company, and Willie had experience of larger stages in long-running melodramas such as Whitbread's *The Irishman* and *Shoulder to Shoulder*. They were later credited with originating the apparently artless 'Abbey style of acting'.

English actors were again engaged in 1900 for Moore's *The Bending of the Bough*, alternating nightly with Martyn's *Maeve* and Alice Milligan's *The Last Feast of the Fianna* at the opulent Gaiety Theatre. The *Irish Theatregoer* deplored having to consult the London press for advance news of these productions, and warned that the Gaiety would be hard to fill – which turned out to be the case. Nonetheless, the ILT again took the Gaiety in October 1901 for *Diarmuid and Grania* by Yeats and Moore, performed by Frank Benson's Shakespearian touring company. This was followed nightly by Douglas Hyde's *Casadh an tSugáin* ('The Twisting of the Rope') by members of the Gaelic League directed by Willie Fay – a curious and prescient contrast.

The writer, painter and social reformer George Russell ('AE') introduced Yeats to the Fay brothers, who were busy with his play *Deirdre*. They agreed to produce Yeats and Gregory's *Cathleen ní Houlihan* at St Theresa's Hall in April 1902, with the revolutionary leader Maude Gonne – idolized by Yeats – as the Old Woman, an evocation of resurgent Ireland. The National Dramatic Society's three performances caused a sensation. Most importantly, Yeats and his associates were at last in touch with enthusiastic and talented Irish actors. Shortly afterwards the group was re-formed as the Irish National Theatre Society, with Yeats as president. The Literary Theatre vanished, but the 'high ambition' and the search for 'that freedom to experiment which is not found in the theatres of England', as articulated in its manifesto of 1898, remained.

Other productions followed in a series of ill-equipped halls. Press reaction was generally patronizing and often destructive. When, in 1903, the Irish Literary Society in London provided the Queen's Gate Hall for performances of Yeats' *The Hour Glass* and *The Pot of Broth*, Gregory's *Twenty-Five*, Yeats and Gregory's *Cathleen ní Houlihan* and JH Cousins' *The Laying of the Foundations*, the reaction from the critics was by contrast hugely encouraging. Miss Horniman, an admirer of Yeats – whose earliest play, *The Land of Heart's Desire*, had been part of her pioneering non-commercial programme at the Avenue Theatre in 1894 – offered not only to design the costumes for Yeats' *The King's Threshold* but also to pay for the Dublin production. Noting the 'hard conditions' in which players and stage staff worked, she told Willie Fay that if a suitable building were found she would contribute enough money for its purchase and renovation. Fay inspected the vacant Mechanics' Theatre, and Miss Horniman accepted the estimate of £1,300 provided by the architect and theatrical enthusiast Joseph Holloway.

While reconstruction was in progress, five highly novel plays were produced elsewhere – *The Shadowy Waters* by Yeats, *The Townland of Tamney* by Seumas MacManus, *In the Shadow of the Glen* and *Riders to the Sea* by JM Synge, and *Broken Soil* by Padraic Colum.

The Synge and Colum works appealed especially to the London critics when the company visited the Royalty Theatre. The clarity of the speaking and unfussy stage business were a source of astonishment and admiration, and it seemed that for the first time in English-language drama since the Middle Ages the hewers of wood and drawers of water were given the leading roles.

As Miss Horniman was not resident in Ireland, the patent for the theatre was made out in the name of Lady Gregory. Miss Horniman wrote to Yeats stating that the building was 'for the use of the National Theatre Society… I can only afford to make a very little theatre and it must be quite simple. You must all do the rest to make it a powerful and prosperous theatre with a high artistic ideal.' As 'stage manager', Willie Fay supervised the work in progress for an annual salary of £70, also paid by Miss Horniman. The stalls contained 178 seats, the pit 186 and the curving balcony 198. The foyer was dimly lighted by two stained-glass windows in peacock colours by Sarah Purser; copper decorations in the neo-Celtic style were designed by the Youghal Art Metal Works. Portraits of Willie Fay, Frank Fay and Miss Horniman by John Butler Yeats, and of the actress Máire ní Shiubhlaigh by Sarah Purser, were in place in the foyer by opening night.

The press was unusually enthusiastic about the building as well as about the two new plays presented, though the *Cork Constitution* observed that 'the theatre has neither orchestra nor bar, and the principal entrance is through a building which was formerly the Dublin morgue'. An orchestra was engaged later, under Dr John F Larchet; the morgue became a favourite topic for gibes. The *Freeman's Journal* paid tribute to Miss Horniman, found that in *On Baile's Strand* Yeats had 'approached somewhat the Shakespearian model without sacrificing his own originality of treatment', and welcomed the 'innocent exaggeration' of Lady Gregory's *Spreading the News* as a change from comedies 'of the blundering stupidity of the *Handy Andy* type'. The playing of Sara Allgood, Máire ni Shiubhlaigh, and Frank and Willie Fay was universally praised.

The *United Irishman* was more cautious and more penetrating. Congratulating the company on its enterprise, it warned against the easy reliance on one-act plays. It also quoted Arthur Griffith (later president of Sinn Fein) to the effect that if the theatre was to live it must 'be moulded by the influences which are moulding National life at present' – a motif which would perennially concentrate debate. On the matter of short plays, Synge's *The Well of the Saints*, then in rehearsal, was written in three substantial acts, and Yeats was in contact with Shaw about a full-length work.

What hindsight discloses is that there was already a growing cleft between plays drawing sustenance from a heroic past and plays of a more mundane present – audiences were less than intrigued by the former. The newly translated cycles of Irish mythology did not find a modern poet with the dramatic flair to bring them to the popular stage as Aeschylus had done so resplendently with the Greek myths. Yeats possessed the vision, and the magicianship with words, but not the large-scale plan. The real tragedy was that Wilde was no longer present. Had he taken on the Deirdre myth in his *Salomé* mode, the theatre would have had a voluptuous work suffused with dark eroticism, glinting with gem-like images, theatrically agitated, dramatic and full-length.

Coole Park, Co Galway, home of the
Gregory family and presided over by
Lady Gregory following the death of
her husband, Sir William Gregory, in
1892. The house became both a retreat
and a workplace for Yeats; many other
writers and artists were made welcome
there, among them JM Synge, George
Bernard Shaw and Sean O'Casey.

The poster for the opening
performance at the Abbey Theatre
on 27 December 1904, establishing
a tradition of bold typefaces and
clear layout.

The first production of Lady Gregory's
Spreading the News, a masterpiece of
simple comic storytelling.

The first production at the Abbey
Theatre of Yeats and Gregory's
Cathleen ní Houlihan in 1904.
Originally performed in St Theresa's
Convent Hall in 1902, it was quickly
absorbed into the Abbey repertoire.

Two first productions by the National
Theatre Society at the Molesworth Hall,
Dublin, in 1903: Yeats' *The King's
Threshold*, with costumes — described
by Lennox Robinson as 'ugly dresses' —
by the theatre's benefactress-to-be
Annie Horniman; and Lady Gregory's
Twenty-Five. The pictures were taken
by the Chancellor Studios in Dublin.

opposite
Olwen Fouéré and David Heap as the shades of the Old Man's father and mother in James Flannery's 1990 production of Yeats' *Purgatory*.

Poster for Lady Gregory's *The Rising of the Moon*, drawn by the actor Philip Guiry while serving as an officer in Flanders during World War I. He was asked to stage an Irish play for the troops, and was able to recall and transcribe the full script.

2

Máire O'Neill (the stage name of
Molly Allgood) as the first Pegeen Mike
in Synge's *The Playboy of the Western
World* in 1907. Playwright and player
were engaged to be married, but
Synge's untimely death intervened.

disgrace, illness and death had successively removed Wilde from even notional participation in the new theatre in his native city. The theatre itself was unable to rise to the technical and casting demands of the only other Irish playwright of international repute, Shaw. Yet a new and entirely original dramatist was revealing himself: John Millington Synge.

Synge's earliest performed play, *In the Shadow of the Glen* (1903), was savaged by the Irish press: if it was (marginally) acceptable that urban Norwegian Protestant Nora Helmer in Ibsen's *A Doll's House* should be seen to make a radical decision about her own life, it was certainly not acceptable for rural Irish Roman Catholic Nora Burke – the play was 'a slur on Irish womanhood'. *Riders to the Sea* (1904) fared better; a tragedy of human helplessness in the hands of destructive nature, there was nothing of a locally contentious nature to criticize, though the *Irish Times* did manage to complain that the drowned boy's corpse on the stage was 'not artistic'. Max Beerbohm was in the vanguard of intellectual opinion when he hailed Synge's early masterpiece in the (London) *Saturday Review*.

Yeats had met this grave young man in Paris, recommending him to seek his themes in the desolate stony places of Ireland rather than the libraries of Europe. Much later, Yeats' claim to having 'discovered' Synge met with some scepticism, but it is certain that without Yeats' exhortation to go to the Aran Islands and live 'as one of the people themselves; express a life that has never found expression', Synge would not have found his true *métier*, and it is unlikely that he would have emerged as the playwright for whom the Irish dramatic movement was searching. After Synge's early death, Yeats was to become, in a sense, the pupil rather than the master.

Synge endowed his herdsmen and vagrants, his publicans and fisherfolk, with a speech that was his own synthesis of Hiberno-English and the richly idiomatic Irish which he absorbed in the homes of the islanders and studied in the publications of the Irish Texts Society and in translations such as the immensely influential *Amhráin Gradha Conachta/Love Songs of Connacht* by Douglas Hyde. Curiously, critics at the time did not perceive that the rhythm and cadence of Synge's dramatic dialogue varies little from character to character and from region to region; what was noted with exclamations varying from hostility and disgust to admiration and wonder was the robustness of expression

fiery and magnificent and tender

and richness of imagery. 'In a good play,' Synge wrote, 'every speech should be as fully flavoured as a nut or an apple… In Ireland, for a few years more, we have a popular imagination that is fiery and magnificent and tender; so that those of us who wish to write start with a chance that is not given to writers where the springtime of the local life has been forgotten.'

The Well of the Saints was the first three-act play to be produced on the Abbey stage. Based on a story from early French literature, it tells of two garrulous blind beggars whose sight is miraculously restored; they witness the villainy of the world, and when their sight dims again they are sustained by their own powerful inner vision. Later playwrights, including Samuel Beckett, acknowledged the influence of this sombre comedy. Audiences at the first production were pitifully small, but Yeats' championing of Synge was vindicated.

The generally dismissive press reaction was mild in comparison to what greeted The Playboy of the Western World two years later. Christy Mahon's gulling of a rural community with his increasingly embroidered tale of parricide, his winning of universal awe and approval, and his exposure as a fraud with its violent outcome, provided ample material for shrill denunciation from most quarters. It seems extraordinary that a play could generate such passion, but the fact is that by the third night fifty policemen were insufficient to quell the disturbance. Several members of the audience were arrested and subsequently fined. The controversy filled the news columns of Irish and British newspapers for several weeks. 'An unmitigated, protracted libel upon Irish peasant men, and worse still upon Irish peasant girlhood,' declared the nationalist (and bourgeois) Freeman's Journal. The unionist press in general found the work vulgar. Lady Gregory, who did not care for the play – she was 'bewildered by its abundance and fantasy' – and Yeats, who privately felt there was too much 'bad language', remained magnificently loyal. He came forward famously on the stage to tell the audience that it had rocked 'the cradle of genius'; his concern was for freedom of speech in the theatre, and he later wrote that Synge was hated 'because he gave his country what it needed'.

It was inevitable that some of those who sought an independent Ireland should have seen the directors of the self-styled 'National' Theatre Society as relics of the colonial regime. All three were Protestant, though from very different backgrounds – Synge from the impoverished landed gentry, Yeats from the middle-class intelligentsia, and Lady Gregory from the Anglo-Irish aristocracy. There was certainly a perception that the directors were the landlords, and the players and staff the peasantry. It was galling for the triumvirate that their idealistic nationalism should be called into question – and also how so many of their unionist relatives believed they had 'gone over to the other side'. Synge was seen as betraying his religion and his class through his relationship with the actress Molly Allgood ('Máire O'Neill') who played Pegeen in the first Playboy.

It was some time before the players felt at ease with The Playboy. A successful English tour later that year, when Synge was hailed as a major dramatist, helped to alleviate doubts, as did news of the first German-language production of The Well of the Saints. A Dublin revival of The Playboy two years later passed without untoward incident.

● ●

As well as public controversy there was internal dissension. In 1905, when Miss Horniman agreed to pay an annual subsidy towards actors' salaries, the supremely talented Máire nic Shiubhlaigh, with six colleagues who favoured the promotion of Irish culture unsullied by commercialism, left the company in order to preserve their amateur status. Later, Miss Horniman's personal antipathy to Willie Fay resulted in her cajoling the triumvirate into agreeing that Fay be confined to working on 'peasant plays', and that an English director be engaged for other genres. Ben Iden Payne did not survive the hornets' nests of Abbey green room and stage for more than a few months, after which Fay requested full control. When this was refused, he, his brother Frank and his wife, the actress Brigid O'Dempsey, resigned. Sara and Molly Allgood and several others remained: they had benefited from Fay's tuition, and they sustained his 'Abbey style' of acting – which became equated with the 'poetic realism' of Synge's plays.

In the six years from the opening of the Abbey Theatre to the death of Synge in 1909, thirty-two new plays appeared. Lady Gregory's folk plays in the 'Kiltartan' dialect were in constant demand; her adaptations from Molière now seem nerveless but at the time they possessed the attraction of experiment. The comparative failure of Yeats' *Deirdre* caused him to admit that his work would 'not draw audiences for a considerable time'. Nonetheless, his heroic farce *The Golden* (later *Green*) *Helmet* showed how the poet was coming to terms with the craft of the stage.

Padraic Colum's genuinely rural voice introduced a sense of contemporaneity. Here were Irish country people seen by one of themselves. *Broken Soil* (1903, rewritten in 1919 as *The Fiddler's House*) deals with the need for the imaginative member of the household, in this case a musician, to move away to avoid spiritual stagnation. In *The Land* (1905) the concern with agrarian problems is carefully subordinated to character and atmosphere. *Thomas Muskerry* (1910) – Balzacian in its delineation of the corrupting power of money – remains his strongest work. Colum's contribution to the development of the repertoire was appreciated by all sections of the curiously compartmentalized Abbey audience.

Yeats was endemically antipathetic to 'realistic' drama; yet when attending a performance of George Fitzmaurice's *The Country Dressmaker* (1907) – which he had reluctantly agreed to accept – he surprised himself when he discovered how well it played and how completely it involved the audience. Some later plays by Fitzmaurice – even those which are fantasies that might have appealed to him – had to wait half a century for production. Fitzmaurice believed that Yeats was jealous of his talent – if this were the case, dozens of other playwrights should have been so affected. A case in point was William Boyle, whose highly accessible dramas of provincial life – *The Building Fund* (1905) and *The Eloquent Dempsey* and *The Mineral Workers* (both 1906) – were given generous space on the Abbey stage and on foreign tours. Yet the question as to whether playwrights – no matter how distinguished – were the right people to select the work of their contemporaries for performance was one which hovered uneasily in the paternalistic ethos of the Abbey Theatre for many years to come.

WG Fay as the Tramp in Synge's
In the Shadow of the Glen at the
Molesworth Hall, Dublin, in 1903.
He also created the part of Christy
Mahon opposite Máire O'Neill in the
first production of *The Playboy of
the Western World*.

JA O'Rourke as the Saint in the first
production of Synge's *The Well of
the Saints* in 1905.

The Tinker's Wedding (1907) was
considered 'too dangerous' for
production at the time of writing,
and was not staged at the Abbey until
the centenary of Synge's birth in 1971.
In this 1985 production directed by
Paul Moore, the cast was Máire ní
Ghráinne, Geoffrey Golden and
Maureen Toal.

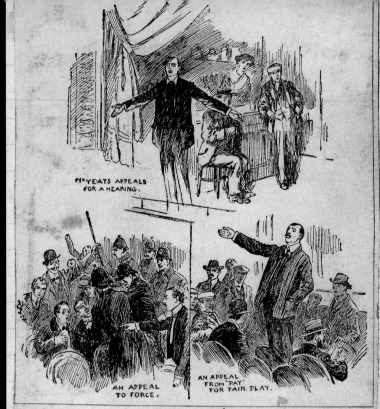

MR. YEATS APPEALS FOR A HEARING.

AN APPEAL TO FORCE.

AN APPEAL FROM "PAT" FOR FAIR PLAY.

ANOTHER INJUSTICE TO IRELAND? THE DISORDERLY SCENES AT A DUBLIN THEATRE DURING THE PRODUCTION OF A PLAY WHICH WAS DISTASTEFUL TO THE AUDIENCE.

Disorderly scenes marked the first performance of "The Playboy of the Western World" at the Abbey Theatre, Dublin, a theatre which is entirely devoted to the production of Irish dramas. The idea of the play is, that the hero, a man who is supposed to have murdered his father, is protected, admired and courted by the women of the Irish village in which he seeks shelter, until it is discovered that his victim was only beaten, and then he is driven from the district by his disgusted admirers. From the time of the rising of the curtain the audience clearly showed that they disliked the play and would have none of it. Cries of "Kill the author!" "The Irish don't protect murderers!" greeted the actors, and not a word spoken on the stage could be heard. Mr. Yates, the managing director of the theatre, appealed in vain to the audience for fair play, but he was received with howls. Patriotic songs were sung in all parts of the house, and the men in the galleries stamped loudly on the floor. The police were called in, and some of the more energetic disturbers were removed.

top
A portrait of JM Synge by the Green Photographic Studio in Dublin. He died at thirty-eight, having achieved greatness for the burgeoning Irish Dramatic Movement.

above
Lady Gregory's nephew, Hugh Lane, ejecting 'rowdies' from a performance of *The Playboy of the Western World*.

A page from *The Graphic* of January 1907 showing 'disorderly scenes' at the third night of Synge's *The Playboy of the Western World*. WB Yeats is depicted as speaking while the actors were still on stage – he informed the audience that they had rocked 'the cradle of genius'. Having delivered his speech to the newspaper offices, he returned to the affray.

opposite
Patrick Mason's majestic production of Synge's *The Well of the Saints* in 1995 reintroduced this sombre comedy to huge audiences in Ireland, Britain and Australia. It was designed by Monica Frawley, with Derry Power as Martin Doul, Pat Leavy as Mary Doul, Derbhle Crotty as Molly Byrne, and Stewart Graham as the Saint.

The earliest known photograph of
a scene from George Fitzmaurice's
rural drama *The Country Dressmaker*.
First performed in 1907, Yeats found
it 'harsh, strong and ugly'. It became
a staple work of the repertoire.
The players in this 1949 revival were
Brian O'Higgins, Bríd Lynch and
Labhrás O Gallchobhair.

opposite
A drawing by Robert Gregory of the
poet and playwright Padraic Colum
(1881–1972), author of some of the
Abbey Theatre's most original folk plays.

Colum
y R Gregory.

on tour abroad

The plays and players who were to coalesce as the National Theatre Society toured outside Ireland as early as 1902; by 1910 tours to leading British theatres were an annual event. *Opposite, top:* The Abbey Players at the Broadway Theatre in Denver, Colorado, in 1932, by which time tours of six months or more were essential to the company's economy. *Middle:* The casts of Tom MacIntyre's *The Great Hunger* (left) and John B Keane's *The Field* pictured by Fergus Bourke in costume in Red Square, Moscow, in 1988. *Left:* Desmond Cave as Yeats' King Oedipus at the Edinburgh Festival in 1973. *This page, left:* Barry McGovern as Clov and Godfrey Quigley as Hamm in Beckett's *Endgame* at the National Theatre in Athens in 1973. *Right:* Eugene O'Brien's atmospheric monologue play *Eden,* directed by Conor McPherson with Don Wycherley and Catherine Walsh in London in 2003.

3

George Bernard Shaw in the kitchen at
Lady Gregory's home, Coole Park, in the
summer of 1915. They discussed plans
for the first production of *John Bull's
Other Island*, and a proposed new play,
O'Flaherty, VC.

The first production of *The Playboy of the Western World*, the departure of the Fay entourage (which caused almost as much public contention) and the death of Synge stand out as markers in the story of the early Abbey Theatre. The Fay style of acting and Synge's legacy of plays defined the work of the company for the outside world. Composed in the idiom that Synge had forged as a new means of expression in the theatre, his unfinished *Deirdre of the Sorrows* was brought to the stage by Lady Gregory and Máire O'Neill in 1910.

Relations with their principal benefactor, Miss Horniman, were already deteriorating when the directors decided to accept George Bernard Shaw's offer of his 'sermon in crude melodrama' *The Shewing-Up of Blanco Posnet*. In London Shaw had been refused a performing licence by the Lord Chamberlain on the grounds of blasphemy. The British censor's remit did not extend to Ireland, but the administration at Dublin Castle had the power to withdraw a theatre's patent, and now threatened to do so. Lady Gregory engaged in a lengthy and painful tussle with the Castle, and the play was produced in spite of serious objections. When asked by a bystander why cheering was heard from the theatre on the opening night, she replied: 'They are defying the Lord Lieutenant!'

If it was hoped that this 'defiance' would improve the theatre's relations with the nationalist press, it had the opposite effect on Miss Horniman, with whom the directors were trying to negotiate favourable terms for the purchase of her lease. Problems were compounded when the new manager, Lennox Robinson, then aged twenty-two, decided to keep the theatre open on the day following the death of King Edward VII – a telegram from Lady Gregory advising closure 'through courtesy' was not delivered in time. The effect on Miss Horniman was catastrophic. She had particularly emphasized that the theatre should not be made use of for political ends, and saw this discourtesy to the monarchy as a further example of the Abbey's attempt to ingratiate itself with 'rebel' opinion. Yeats refused to dismiss Robinson. An unseemly legal and financial quarrel ensued, observed with glee by those who detected personal motives – a jealous Miss Horniman was seen to have lost significant ground to Lady Gregory in the matter of Yeats' friendship. Finally, Miss Horniman agreed to relinquish the patent to her rival, but she discontinued her annual subsidy.

Lady Gregory took up the additional task of fundraising. London, where the company's productions always impressed audiences and critics, seemed the most likely source. Events were organized over a long

● ●

commercial realities

period, the most beneficial being a series of lectures by Gregory, Yeats, Shaw and St John Ervine arranged by the Irish impresario JB Fagan who, as a young man, had written *The Rebels*, one of the successful melodramas of which the founders of the Irish Literary Theatre so strenuously disapproved.

In 1911 it was decided to accept the offer of a New York agent for a tour of the United States. The plays chosen were five well-established pieces by Lady Gregory, *Spreading the News*, *Hyacinth Halvey*, *The Jackdaw*, *The Workhouse Ward* and *MacDaragh's Wife*; Yeats and Gregory's *Cathleen ní Houlihan*; Synge's *In the Shadow of the Glen*, *The Well of the Saints* and *The Playboy of the Western World*; Shaw's *The Shewing-Up of Blanco Posnet*; Boyle's *The Mineral Workers*; two plays by the young Lennox Robinson, *The Clancy Name* and *Harvest*; and one by the recently discovered TC Murray, *Birthright*. The list is interesting for what was included – clearly there was a risk involved with Synge's plays – just as it is for what was not: not one of Yeats' verse plays, nor any on a subject taken from pre-Christian mythology.

Thirty-one cities were visited, the players being absent from home for almost five months. Among those who saw all the plays was the twenty-three-year-old Eugene O'Neill, who later said that the Abbey provided 'a glimpse of my opportunity', Murray's *Birthright* and Synge's *Playboy* creating the deepest impression on him. The reception from regular American theatregoers was rapturous; but the Irish immigré sector was not to be blandished by highfalutin notions of dramatic art: what was seen on the stage was an Ireland that they did not wish to remember. The United Gaelic Society of New York resolved 'to drive this vile thing [*The Playboy*] from the stage'. Yeats' talks in defence of the play were well reported, but there were organized protests in Providence and New Haven, while in Philadelphia the entire cast was arrested on a charge of corruption. Lady Gregory's New York friend, the lawyer and art patron John Quinn, defended *The Playboy* brilliantly; the actors were released on bail and in Pittsburgh later learned that the case had been dismissed.

Two other equally arduous, but less problematic, tours followed. The purpose was to make money to keep the theatre going at home – but at home there was considerable irritation over the protracted absence of leading players, and dissatisfaction at the standard of the productions that were left to occupy the stage. A tour of large English theatres – including the 2,358-seat London Coliseum – was seen as detrimental to the Abbey's traditionally intimate style of performance.

When Sara Allgood and Máire O'Neill left the company in 1913 to fulfil commercial engagements, theirs seemed like a defection of the magnitude of the Fays' – but the vacuum was filled by burgeoning talent, and many who were seen as 'forsaking' the Abbey would keep returning. Producers and managers came and went with even greater rapidity, the pressures from an autocratic board, fractious staff, volatile audience and hostile press, as well as long hours and low pay, taking their toll. The English director Nugent Monck brought a temporary improvement in production standards, but his penchant for poetic and liturgical drama failed to draw the crowds. He made use of the much-spoken-of but little-seen screens which had been designed by Edward Gordon Craig for the plays of

Yeats, engaging Craig to design costumes and masks for revivals of *The Hour Glass* and *On Baile's Strand*, and he employed Charles Ricketts to design costumes for a new production of *The Well of the Saints* – thus many of the early plays were seen in more interesting guise.

Save the prentice authorship of two plays, Lennox Robinson had no training of any kind when Yeats and Lady Gregory appointed him manager and producer in 1909. He weathered several dismissals, resignations and reappointments; when he died in 1958 he was still a member of the board. He was always held in much affection as the Abbey Theatre's eccentric public face. His earliest major success as a playwright came in 1916 with *The Whiteheaded Boy*, the quintessential comedy of small town life in which vexing domestic issues never turn out quite as the participants would wish. Robinson's use of ironic narration was novel at the time.

Robinson resigned his managerial duties when the US–Canadian tour of 1914 lost money. He was replaced by A Patrick Wilson and then, temporarily, by the actor Udolphus Wright prior to the appointment of the Belfast playwright St John Greer Ervine. Ervine's *Mixed Marriage* (1911) is the earliest in the long line of Ulster plays on sectarian issues which continues into the twenty-first century. It rattled a drum of recognition when the Abbey gave it at the Grand Opera House, Belfast. Ervine's most enduring Abbey play is *John Ferguson* (1915), which traces the declining fortunes of a respectable Presbyterian family into a marriage of convenience and two squalid *crimes passionels*.

Ervine managed to place the theatre's finances on a firmer base. He found the members of the company to be lacking in discipline and motivation, injudiciously comparing them with the men and women who volunteered for wartime service in 1914–18. After a series of unpleasant confrontations the actors refused to perform, and several departed to create yet another offshoot company, presenting the popular Abbey plays abroad – much to the confusion of audiences who believed they were seeing the official Abbey. These developments took place around the time of the Easter Rising of 1916, in which a number of players and staff took an active part and which Ervine viewed with disdain, referring to one of the leaders, Eamon de Valéra, as 'a damned dago'. He lost little time in resigning his post to join the army. He later became drama critic for the *Observer*, a successful West End playwright, and the biographer of Wilde and Shaw. In 1936 he gave his Ulster comedy, *Boyd's Shop*, to the Abbey, but only after it had first been performed in Liverpool.

Shortly after Ervine's resignation it was decided to produce *John Bull's Other Island*, the play commissioned from Shaw in 1904 but as yet unproduced at the Abbey. Granville Barker's company had given it in Dublin in the meantime with enormous success. Such was the public delight in the sheer effervescence of the piece that for the next fifteen years it was repeated annually. Shaw enjoyed an intense period of acclaim under the new producer J Augustus Keogh, who presented no fewer than six of his existing plays during the 1916–17 season; but *O'Flaherty VC*, a short comedy on military recruitment in Ireland which Yeats and Lady Gregory had requested from him, was not performed because the topic was felt to be too sensitive at a time when thousands of young Irishmen were dying in the trenches in Flanders.

Sold by the Irish Players at £1.00
towards a building to save Sir Hugh Lane's Great Gift of
Pictures for Ireland
April 1913

Look up in the sun's eye, and give
What the exalted heart calls good,
That some new day may breed the best,
Because you gave, not what they would,
But the right twigs for an eagle's nest.

"Michael Cooney: 'There is the use of calling it a lend, when I
know I never will see it again?' 'It might as well earn me
the value of a charity.'"

Irish Theatre Company

Abbey
Theatre
May 26 –
June 14
8.00 pm

John
Bull's
Other
Island

A comedy by
George Bernard
Shaw

above
Decorated handkerchief with scenes
from GB Shaw's *The Shewing-Up of
Blanco Posnet*, a fundraising memento
for the proposed gallery to house Sir
Hugh Lane's collection of modern
paintings and sculpture. The play had
been banned in England, and its Abbey
Theatre production was exceptionally
controversial.

top right
John Bull's Other Island, commissioned
in 1904 but not produced at the Abbey
until 1916. In 1981 the authorities in
Belfast required the removal of the
national flags from the Irish Theatre
Company's caricature poster; in Glasgow
the flags were allowed – provided they
were not printed in colour!

above
TC Murray provided the Abbey Theatre
with a series of powerfully realistic
plays set in the Munster countryside
between 1910 and 1939. His work had
a deep influence on the young Eugene
O'Neill.

Eileen O'Doherty acted in the first
productions of two of TC Murray's
plays, *Birthright* and *Maurice Harte*.
Between 1907 and 1912 she created
over a dozen roles in works by almost
as many writers, as well as appearing
in several revivals.

Corner of Abbey Street, Dublin.

Abbey Street, Dublin, as seen by
theatre staff and members of the
public following bombardment from
the British gunboat *Helga* during
Easter Week, 1916. The theatre
building was out of the line of fire.

opposite
A page from the box-office accounts book
for the spring of 1916. The blank space
indicates the theatre's closure in the
week of the Easter Rising. The play was
to have been TH Nally's appropriately
titled *The Spancel of Death*. It was never
resurrected at the Abbey.

28/2/16 2 ins 24/-
29/2/16 1/2 — 17/
1/3/16 1/2 — 17/
2/3/16 1/2 — 17/
3/3/16 1/2 — 17/
4/3/16 1/2 — 14/
Paid 6/3/16 — 3 - 12.0

6/3/16 1 1/2 ins 12/-
7/3/16 12/-
8/3/16 12/-
9/3/16 12/-
10/3/16 12/-
11/3/16 12/-
Paid 14/3/16 3 - 12

13/3/16 1 1/2 ins 14/-
14/3/16 14/-
15/3/16 10/-
16/3/16 10/-
17/3/16 10/-
18/3/16 8/-
Paid 2/3/16 2 - 18.0

20/3/16 1 1/4 10/-
21/3/16 1 1/2 10/-
22/3/16 10/-
23/3/16 10/-
24/3/16 10/-
25/3/16 3 0.0
Paid 27/3/16 12/-
28/3/16 12/-
29/3/16 12/-
30/3/16 12/-
31/3/16 12/-
1st April 1 1/4 12/-
Musical Rec 3 - 12 0
Paid 4/4/16

Sunday Musical Recitals
4 insertions @ 8/- = 1.12.0 Paid 2/3/16

30/3/16 1 in 8/-
31/3/16 8/-
1/4/16 8/-
1.4.0
Paid 4/4/16

6/4/16 1 in 8/-
7/4/16 8/-
8/4/16 8/-
1.4.0
Paid 11/4/16

15/4/16 1/2 12/-
16/4/16 1/2 12/-
1.4.0
Paid 18/4/16

17/4/16 16/-
18/4/16 16/-
19/4/16 16/-
20/4/16 16/-
21/4/16 16/-
22/4/16 16/-
23/4/16
24/4/16 14/-
25/4/16 11/4
26/4/16 11/4
27/4/16
28/4/16
29/4/16
6.14-8
Paid 16/5/16

8 — may — 1 in — 8/
9 — 1 — 8/
10 — 1 — 8/
11 — 1 — 8/
12 — 1 — 8/
13 — 1 — 8/
Paid 16/5/16 2 - 8.0

10 — 2 in — 16/
11 — 2 — 16/
12 — 2 — 16/
13 — 2 — 16/
Paid 16/5/16 3 4 Proper a/c.

18/5/16 1 1/2 ins — 17/
19/5/16 — 17/
20/5/16 — 17/
21/5/16 — 17/
22/5/16 1/2 = 17/
23/5/16 1/2 17/
24/5/16 1/2 17/
25/5/16 1/2 17/
26/5/16 1/2 17/
27/5/16 1/2 17/
Paid 30/5/16 3 - 12

29/5/16 — 1/2 — 17/
Paid 31/5/16

Abbey Theatre Lettering

Poster designed by Augustus John
in 1921 as the artist's contribution
to a number of fundraising schemes
at a time when the theatre's financial
position was causing much anxiety.
Three years later the government
agreed an annual subsidy.

opposite
Micheál MacLíammóir, co-founder
of the Dublin Gate Theatre, designed
the poster for Mary Manning's
dramatization of Frank O'Connor's
novel *The Saint and Mary Kate* in 1968.

The Saint and Mary Kate

by Frank O'Connor and Mary Manning

THE ABBEY THEATRE

Mich... mac Liammóir

above
Watercolour by Jack B Yeats, RHA,
showing the interior of the Mechanics'
Theatre prior to its becoming the Abbey
Theatre. The play is a melodrama based
on William Carleton's novel of 1855
Willy Reilly and his Dear Colleen Bawn.

opposite
Costume design by Charles Ricketts
for the 1917 revival of Yeats' *On Baile's
Strand*. This is the hero Cuchulain's
sea-cloak which is left on stage in
a pool of light after he has rushed
out to die fighting the waves.

overleaf
Costumes by Tanya Moiseiwitsch for
Douglas Hyde's *Casadh an tSugáin*
in 1938, the play's first major revival
since the Irish Literary Theatre/Gaelic
League premiere in 1901. The players
for whom these costumes were designed
were Bríd Lynch, Moya Devlin, Phyllis
Ryan and Shelah Ward.

Lynch

Devlin

Ryan   Ward

clockwise from bottom left
Frank Fay (1870–1931), who was largely
responsible for creating the economic
style of production for which the Abbey
became famous; noted for his speaking
of verse, he appeared in several of Yeats'
early plays. Annie Horniman (1860–1937),
the English tea heiress who provided
essential financial support to the
company in its early years and paid for
the renovation of the theatre. Máire
O'Neill (1885–1952), who created many
leading roles including Pegeen Mike in
The Playboy of the Western World. These
now celebrated images by John Butler
Yeats are in the Abbey Theatre Portrait
Collection, as is the painting of WB
Yeats (1865–1939) by Sean O'Sullivan.

Bronze head of Lady Gregory
by Jacob Epstein, RA, in the Hugh Lane
Municipal Gallery of Modern Art.

Caricature by Grace Plunkett of
Rutherford Mayne (*né* Samuel Waddell)
in the title role of *The Emperor Jones*
by Eugene O'Neill in 1927. Mayne
wrote three plays which were first
performed at the Abbey Theatre,
Bridgehead (1934) being an outstanding
success. His acting was less admired.

4

Robert Ballagh's portrait of
Sean O'Casey.

If the Abbey Theatre experienced its lowest ebb of morale during the period which lasted from the Easter Rising of 1916 until the establishment of the Irish Free State in 1922, the same might be said of the entire country. In practical terms, the uncertainty of the military situation meant that patrons were unwilling to risk 'evenings out' at any theatre. It was more difficult for the Abbey because the early performances required by frequent curfews meant that the part-time actors, on whom the company still partially relied, were not available. Permanent players were obliged to accept a third of their usual salaries. During the Anglo–Irish War of 1919–21 the situation became unsustainable, and the theatre was forced to suspend performances for weeks at a time.

Support from various sources was probably more helpful morally than financially. Sara Allgood, with former Abbey actors who were appearing in Fagan's production of Robinsons's *The Whiteheaded Boy* in London, organized a 'rescue' matinée. St John Ervine, somewhat surprisingly, wrote a coolly appreciative piece in the *Observer* claiming that the Abbey was now 'the oldest and most vital repertory theatre in these islands'. Irish newspapers gave unusually generous space to interviews designed to encourage fundraising – Lennox Robinson, in the *Freeman's Journal*, declared

that subscriptions were not being actively canvassed in Ireland 'because of the existing want and distress', yet several generous Irish subscriptions were received. The *Irish Independent* made the point that 'when the Abbey is gone, the Mirror of Ireland is broken, and not for a long time can we again see our sins or our virtues… reflected so truthfully or so honestly'. Such sentiments were as manna to directors and players, used as they were to journalistic disparagement, but sporadic revivals of popular plays, and first productions of fine work by George Shiels, J Bernard McCarthy, Rutherford Mayne and Brinsley Macnamara, did not sell enough seats; even the return of Frank Fay and other early luminaries failed to entice a jittery clientele.

The Anglo–Irish Treaty was approved by Dáil Eireann (the Irish parliament) in January 1922. The constitution of the Irish Free State was adopted in October, but as early as April Lennox Robinson was claiming that it had always been the directors' intention 'to hand the Abbey Theatre over to the Irish Government'. In a well-reasoned memorandum he stressed the importance universally placed on the concept of a National Theatre 'except in England and its colonies, the United States and Venezuela', and the desirability of forming 'a company of Gaelic players' on account of 'the Government's known desire to build on Gaelic

our theatre seems indestructible

civilization'. Informal talks took place over the next two years – an alarmed minister for education told Lady Gregory he was 'sure the new Government did not wish to manage a theatre!' It was not until June 1924 that Lady Gregory addressed a request for financial aid to President William T Cosgrave. This reached the minister for finance, Ernest Blythe, and eventually a revenue grant of £850 was announced on 4 August 1925.

A number of disparate factors had clearly helped. Of these, the interest of Ernest Blythe was most crucial. A Methodist from Magheragall, Co Antrim, Blythe possessed the dedicated enthusiasm of the discoverer of Gaelic culture, and saw that the Abbey could become an important cog in the machinery of the language revival. Yeats – correctly viewed as the theatre's inspirational force – had already been appointed to the Irish Senate; his Nobel Prize for Literature in 1923 bathed the tyro nation in an effulgence of artistic glory. There also was the appearance of a new playwright who at the age of forty-two drew immediate attention: Sean O'Casey.

O'Casey (*né* John Casey) came from a shabby-genteel urban Protestant background. In early life he embraced a succession of seemingly contradictory causes, socialism becoming the dominant and most enduring. Intense reading, and involvement in amateur drama, led him to playwriting and the Abbey, where Lady Gregory shrewdly encouraged him by turning down early attempts and advising him to develop his 'peculiar gift for character-drawing'. *The Shadow of a Gunman* (1923) is a series of humorous character sketches held together by a tenuous plot; the 'gunman' of the title is locally admired as a hero but is in fact an impostor. The fact that the play is set in a poverty-ridden tenement against a background of the guerrilla fighting of only three years previously between Sinn Fein and the Auxiliaries (the notorious 'Black-and-Tans') added an extraordinary piquancy. In *Juno and the Paycock* (1924) the divided Boyle family may be seen to stand for the Ireland of the profoundly dehumanizing Civil War of 1922–23. The mother figure, Juno, as in the classical myth, is exalted as the ultimate source of courage and responsibility; the eponymous 'paycock' is her strutting loud-mouthed husband. The play is a hymn to the courage and responsibility of great-hearted women in the face of the unthinking vanity of the male.

The folly and waste of war, and the insincerity of sentimental patriotism, are themes which also suffuse *The Plough and the Stars* (1926). Some observers, including members of the original casts, felt that these plays would be forgotten once they ceased to be topical, but there is a universality of compassion in O'Casey's vision of human suffering and resilience, and he had created a new genre of tragic satire in which to express it. It is not surprising that many members of the first audiences at *The Plough and the Stars* found what seemed to them to be O'Casey's mocking view of Irish nationalism exceptionally offensive. By the third night there were disturbances in the theatre reminiscent of those which had attended the birth of Synge's *Playboy*. The real 'reasons' for the riots were not so much the presence on stage (for example) of a prostitute, or the pastiche of Padraic Pearse's oration at the grave of the Fenian leader O'Donovan Rossa, but more that the 1916 Rising was depicted with photographic realism and not as an idealized patriotic print in sepia tones.

Yeats again rose to the significance of the moment: he told a nervous actor, Gabriel Fallon, that he had sent for the police – 'and this time it will be their own police!' To the outraged assembly he declared: 'You have disgraced yourselves again! … This is O'Casey's apotheosis!' The public controversy continued for several weeks, much to the benefit of the Abbey's box office. O'Casey moved to London, where Fagan's production of *Juno* was the triumph of the season. Two years later he sent the Abbey the script of what he believed to be his best play to date, *The Silver Tassie*. (The 'tassie' is the sporting trophy which the principal character, permanently maimed in the Great War, crushes in a symbolic gesture.) Inconsistency of style and an intractable third act are faults: but these can be overcome in production, and as a stage evocation of the horror of war the play is unsurpassed.

There were excellent reasons for the Abbey directors to produce *The Silver Tassie* – and not only as a mark of gratitude to the author who had placed their theatre back on the international map. Its rejection caused permanent anguish to O'Casey, and – after she saw CB Cochrane's London production – abiding remorse for Lady Gregory. The chief difficulty was Yeats' antipathy to 'expressionism'. In fact, neither he nor Lady Gregory believed that the scene in the trenches, which requires ritualistic movement and choric speaking, was stageable. Furthermore, Yeats had grown towards a curious forgetfulness of the contribution of Irish men and women to the British army in 1914–18.

Another major error of judgment was made in 1927 with the rejection of *Shadowdance*, Denis Johnston's poetic satire on the hucksterish Free State's usurping of the idealism of the national movement. This was also in the dreaded expressionist mode – but this time the Abbey gave the new Gate Theatre Studio house-room for its first production, under the ironic title *The Old Lady Says 'No!'*, in the 101-seat Peacock Theatre. The Peacock was opened in 1926 as the company's second performing space. It became the home of the Abbey School of Acting and, for five years, the Abbey School of Ballet. Some productions by the Dublin Drama League – founded by Yeats and Robinson to introduce modern European and American plays to Dublin – also took place there.

In the historical context O'Casey's plays dominate the revolutionary period, yet there was an abundance of other new plays in a variety of styles and on a remarkable range of topics. Among these were TC Murray's searing *Autumn Fire* (1924), an O'Neill-like drama of familial passions; Lennox Robinson's quasi-Chekhovian *The Big House* (1926), which vividly illuminates the dilemma of the Anglo-Irish country gentry in the new state; the same author's richly comic *The Far-Off Hills* (1928); and Yeats' superb version of *King Oedipus* (1925). Sophocles' tragedy has never been so resoundingly rendered into English, nor with such economy of poetic utterance; here, with its ready-made template, Yeats' stage work steps outside the frame of arcane coterie drama.

The Abbey Theatre seemed to have come through its *Walpurgisnacht* of economic and operational terrors – though there would be more. For the moment, however, it was possible for Lennox Robinson to exclaim: 'Our theatre seems indestructible!'

FJ McCormick and Barry Fitzgerald, two
of O'Casey's most famous interpreters,
in the Abbey foyer on their return from
Hollywood. McCormick created Joxer
Daly in *Juno and the Paycock* and Jack
Clitheroe in *The Plough and the Stars*;
similarly, Fitzgerald created Jack Boyle
and Fluther Good. Both had extensive
screen careers.

Tomás MacAnna's Golden Jubilee
production of *The Plough and the Stars*
in 1976, designed by Bronwen Casson,
with Angela Newman, Siobhán McKenna,
John Kavanagh and Cyril Cusack. This
production later played in New York,
Philadelphia, Boston and Washington, DC.

overleaf left
During the 1970s Tomás MacAnna
directed several of O'Casey's later plays
which had been produced initially
elsewhere, with spectacular effects of
design and movement. Among the cast of
his 1975 production of *Purple Dust* were
Philip O'Flynn, Desmond Cave, Patrick
Laffan, and (seated) Robert Carlyle.

overleaf right
Having rejected *The Silver Tassie*, O'Casey's
compassionate and angry World War I
play, in 1928, in 1935 the Abbey attempted
restitution with an apparently inadequate
staging. Hugh Hunt's 1972 staging,
designed by Alan Barlow, is now seen as
a landmark. John Kavanagh played the
Croucher in the expressionistic second act.

The Shadow of a Gunman, a comedy of tragic ironies set during the Anglo–Irish war of 1922, was O'Casey's earliest work to reach the Abbey stage. In Tomás MacAnna's 1989 production, designed by Wendy Shea, Desmond Cave played the 'gunman' and Martina Stanley the genuinely brave Minnie Powell.

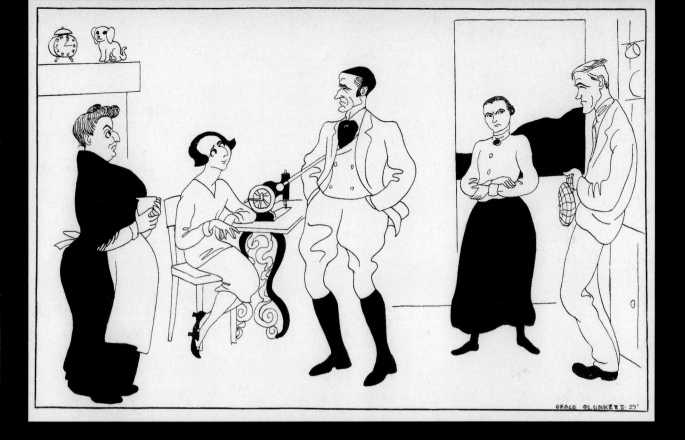

Grace Plunkett's caricatures enlivened
the newpapers of the 1920s and '30s,
extracting fun from the most profoundly
solemn moments. This is her response
to TC Murray's *Autumn Fire* (1924),
where the cast was Maureen Delany,
Eileen Crowe, MJ Dolan, Sara Allgood
and Arthur Shields.

The cast of George Shiels' comedy
The New Gossoon (1930) as seen by
Grace Plunkett: Maureen Delany,
FJ McCormick, Denis O'Dea, Eileen
Crowe and PJ Carolan. This was the
era of the Abbey Players at their most
versatile.

Members of the cast of the first
production of George Shiels' Ulster
comedy *Professor Tim* outside the
theatre in 1925.

In order to extend its range of productions, the National Theatre Society included in its objectives the possibility of 'producing such dramatic works by foreign authors as would tend to educate and interest the public of this country'. *Opposite: Macbeth* has been the Abbey's most frequently produced Shakespeare play: Ray McAnally and Angela Newman took the leading roles in the 1971 production; the costumes were by Bronwen Casson. *Above:* Tomás MacAnna directed *A Midsummer Night's Dream* in 1979, with Fedelma Cullen as Titania, Clive Geraghty as Oberon and John Olohan as Puck, designed by Bronwen Casson.

Above: Joe Dowling directed several Shakespeare plays in the 1970s and '80s, among them *Much Ado about Nothing,* also designed by Bronwen Casson. *Opposite, clockwise from top left:* The distinguished playwright and filmmaker Gerry Stembridge directed *The Comedy of Errors* in 1993. Michael Bogdanov was guest director in 1983 for *Hamlet,* set in a twentieth-century Fascist state, with Godfrey Quigley as the Player King (above) and Stephen Brennan as Hamlet (below). Liam Neeson and Dermot Tuohy are seen here in Patrick Mason's production of *The Winter's Tale* in 1980.

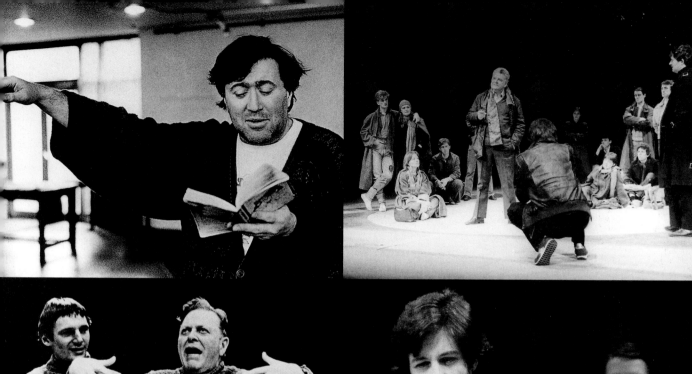

5

For half a century from 1908, Lennox
Robinson (1886–1958) served the Abbey
Theatre as the author of twenty plays,
as producer and as a member of the
board. Dependency on alcohol
occasionally affected his administrative
duties but failed to extinguish his
brilliant gift for playwriting.

the 1930s at the Abbey have been dismissed by the majority of later critics, mainly, it would seem, because no new Synge or O'Casey emerged: yet playwrights of that order are rare in any theatre. Lady Gregory died in 1932. She had not taken an active part in the day-to-day running of the theatre for several years. Of her portrait by Mancini, Yeats memorably wrote: 'But where is the brush that could show anything/ Of all that pride and that humility?' The actor Arthur Sinclair described her as 'very vindictive, narrow-minded and egotistical'. Yeats himself was in failing health, yet of vigorous mind. George Shiels, who would emerge as the most frequently performed playwright of the decade – surpassing O'Casey in sheer public appeal – wrote of the Abbey board members that 'the competition at present is for Yeats' mantle, which must shortly fall from his shoulders'; but Yeats returned periodically from hibernation on the Mediterranean coast to cajole, admonish and, at times, excoriate.

Two of Yeats' most disturbing plays, *The Words upon the Window Pane* (1930) and *Purgatory* (1938), were produced. John F Larchet composed the music for his *The Cat and the Moon* and *The Dreaming of the Bones* (both 1931). Yeats dedicated *The King of the Great Clock Tower* (1935) to Ninette de Valois, 'asking pardon for covering her expressive face with a mask'. Miss de Valois, who was born and brought up in Co Wicklow and had danced with Diaghilev's company, ran the Abbey School of Ballet part-time from 1927 until 1933, when her commitment to the Sadler's Wells Theatre Ballet became a priority.

The conceptual polarities, constantly discussed at the boardroom table and in the press, were a theatre of ideas, where plays should excite the mind and stimulate the imagination, and a populist theatre, where an audience in tune with the practices and precepts of the new state would gather to enjoy an evening's entertainment without too severe an expense of mental effort. Time has shown that those who supported the more 'intellectual' or 'artistic' way have retained a place in literary and dramatic history, while those who favoured the more democratic approach have been forgotten, and are certainly unheard of outside Ireland.

There were political pressures. The general election of 1932 removed the Cosgrave government in which Ernest Blythe was minister for finance,

theatre of ideas or populist theatre?

substituting the first Fianna Fáil regime with Eamon de Valéra as Taoiseach. Yeats invited Blythe to join the theatre's board, partly in recognition of his support in the past and partly because Blythe could still patrol the fiscal corridors; he remained on the board for thirty-seven years. De Valéra's disastrous Economic War with Britain resulted in a reduction in state spending; one casualty was the Abbey's annual grant, which was reduced to a paltry £750. Complaints made to de Valéra by influential Irish-American groups about the detrimental image of Ireland projected on the Abbey tours provoked an awkward stand-off between the government and the National Theatre Society. Yeats' view was that the theatre should dispense with subsidy rather than accept official censorship. Eventually Yeats and de Valéra met, and it was agreed that a note should appear in American touring programmes stating that the government took no responsibility for the plays selected by the subsidized theatre. Of his meeting with de Valéra, Yeats wrote: 'I was impressed by his simplicity and honesty, though we differed throughout.'

Newcomers to the board in 1935 were the poet FR Higgins and the playwright Brinsley Macnamara. The latter's term was brief, for he felt compelled to resign in the face of criticism from devout Roman Catholics when the board at length decided to present O'Casey's *The Silver Tassie*. Macnamara raised the ire of members when he stated publicly that as he was the complainants' only co-religionist on the board he would have been outvoted. The players were incensed because of their lately admitted devotion to O'Casey, whose work was now their bread and butter.

Macnamara failed to apologize. He was not nominated to the opportunistically created management committee, and this forced his departure. The affray was one of many which were given prominence in the press, but there were many which were not: at a meeting when Yeats and Frank O'Connor – then becoming known internationally as one of Ireland's foremost writers of prose fiction – were absent, an anxious board rejected Yeats' *The Herne's Egg* because it was thought to be 'obscene'. This occasioned Blythe's oft-quoted aside that it was so *obscure* no one would notice that it was *obscene*. The board also rejected Paul Vincent Carroll's *The White Steed* in the belief that it might be interpreted as 'anti-clerical'. The increasing narrowness of outlook reached its apogee of absurdity when O'Connor was manoeuvred out of board membership in 1939 because of an indiscreet affair with an English actress and (it was said) his unorthodox views on divorce.

Ever since the production by the Dublin Gate Theatre Studio of Denis Johnston's *The Old Lady Says 'No!'* in 1929, the Gate's star had risen in public estimation. In 1930 its founders, Hilton Edwards and Mícheál MacLíammóir, opened their own theatre, presenting mainly contemporary European and American plays. The Gate's high production values were consistently praised by critics, the Abbey emerging unfavourably by comparison. An amused Denis Johnston wrote of the Abbey having but two stage sets: the 'rural cottage interior' in which the position of door, window and hearth could be alternated from peasant play to peasant play; and the 'wallpaper set', where a hasty pasting prior to dress rehearsal gave a supposedly new appearance to the required urban scene.

The Gate effectively saw off the Abbey-inspired Dublin Drama League, which had similar aims. In response to quite palpable anxiety about the new 'rival' theatre, the Abbey board decided in 1934 to engage the English director Bladon Peake to present a series of foreign plays. This ill-considered attempt to beat the Gate at its own game was strongly opposed by Frank O'Connor, and the hapless Peake's contract was terminated. The fact was, directors of real talent did not exist in Ireland, other than those who – like the Abbey's Arthur Shields and MJ Dolan – were more useful to the company as actors. Lennox Robinson had declined into alcoholism, though this did not appear to affect his playwriting. Yeats put forward the name of another English director: Hugh Hunt. Hunt accepted the position, and his request that Tanya Moiseiwitsch be engaged as designer was agreed to. Within a few months the notion of regular productions of non-Irish plays was abandoned. To Frank O'Connor's surprise and delight, a lively period of creativity ensued.

In his eagerness to revitalize the theatre's inherited repertoire, Hugh Hunt inevitably upset those who believed that established plays must be preserved as replicas of their original productions. The more realistic (or 'less poetic') style of Hunt's 1936 revival of *The Playboy of the Western World,* with Cyril Cusack and other novice players in the cast, caused board outrage – good box-office returns did not convince the members that an alternative approach should quite possibly be welcomed. Hunt's production of Yeats' *Deirdre* displeased because the manner of

delivery of the lines failed to accord with Yeats' ideas on verse-speaking – described by some as 'a drone'. The players were annoyed when Hunt engaged Jean Forbes Robertson and Micheál MacLíammóir as 'stars' for this play, instead of casting from within the company. As a result Hunt was requested not to direct further revivals of Synge and Yeats, a request somewhat capriciously ignored by Yeats himself only two years later when he invited Hunt to direct the first production of *Purgatory*. Hunt, who later admitted that he was 'deflated' by these proceedings, turned to 'the direction of the new plays which were now flooding into the theatre'. In fact, he directed twenty-eight new scripts in three years, among them Frank O'Connor's *The Invincibles* (1937), *In the Train* and *Moses' Rock* (both 1938), Hunt collaborating to a greater or lesser extent on the writing of all three.

The actress Ria Mooney, who had first drawn attention as the prostitute in *The Plough and the Stars* in 1926 and had subsequently enjoyed several years of freelance acting and directing abroad, rejoined the company in Atlanta, Georgia, in 1932. She also went on the American tours which lasted from September 1934 to April 1935 and August 1937 to April 1938 – excessively lengthy engagements that were essential to the theatre's financial survival. When at home, she taught in the School of Acting, and in April 1937 she founded the Abbey Experimental Theatre, a co-operative whose members paid a small subscription towards running costs and had the use of the Peacock Theatre free of charge. They directed and designed their own productions and undertook the administration. Among those who emerged from this

venture to make their names on the Abbey stage –
and also in the theatre and cinema abroad – were
Wilfred Brambell, Dermot Kelly and Jack McGowran.
The Experimental Theatre continued into the 1940s,
by which time Ria Mooney was the Abbey's resident
producer.

In 1938 the board decided to present a festival
of eighteen plays from the repertoire in a series
of matinées and evening performances crammed
into two weeks, as well as one new play, Yeats'
extraordinary *Purgatory*. The festival may be seen as
a final tribute to Yeats, who, as it turned out, died six
months later. The architectural historian Maurice
Craig, present as a student, later recalled that, at the
fall of the curtain after *Purgatory*, 'Yeats moved slowly
from his seat in the stalls, up the steps on the right of
the stage and slowly across to the centre: a figure not
to be forgotten'. His daughter, Anne, who was at this
time assisting Tanya Moiseiwitsch, designed the sets
for *Purgatory* and *On Baile's Strand*. During the
fortnight, Cyril Cusack appeared in nine plays, Arthur
Shields in eight, FJ McCormick and others in seven.
Never, before or since, have the mentally retentive and
physically energetic powers of individual members of
the acting company been so taxed, or so splendidly
demonstrated.

One of the plays revived for the festival was *The
New Gossoon* (1930) by George Shiels. Confined to
a wheelchair, Shiels spent his writing life in his native
Co Antrim, only attending one of the twenty-six of his
plays which were first produced by the Abbey
(*Professor Tim* on tour in Belfast). O'Casey praised
Shiels' characterization and dialogue, but felt that

his enforced absence from the production process
militated against a real understanding of stagecraft.
An acute observer of human frailties and the
possessor of a sharp ear for racy Ulster language,
his early comedies are of small consequence, but *The
New Gossoon,* in its delineation of a heartless young
man intent on the rejection of traditional rural
pieties, showed him to be an astute commentator on
contemporary social change.

All Shiels' plays appear to have been directed in
the naturalistic style for which the Abbey Theatre was
now famous: a tendency in much of his writing
towards a kind of surreal farce seems to have been
ignored. His masterpiece is *The Passing Day* (1936),
in which he presents the figure of a Molièresque
tyrant – a small-town *commerçant* called John Fibbs
– and pursues the theme of domestic meanness
in a startlingly ruthless way. Tyrone Guthrie, who
described Shiels as 'the world's most underrated
dramatist', directed the 1951 Festival of Britain
production in an abstract setting by Tanya
Moiseiwitsch, for the first and probably only time
bringing out the play's essential grotesqueness. This
quality is also essential to *Neal Maquade* (1938) – later
retitled *Macook's Corner* – in which Shiels exposes
a thieves' kitchen of venality and intrigue.

Boyd's Shop (1936), St John Ervine's archetypal
comedy of ambition and cunning set in a rural Ulster
community, like Shiels' *The Passing Day* of the same
year, has suffered at the hands of amateur groups
who produce it as kitchen comedy. (In spite of the
presence of a duplicitous Presbyterian minister in
Boyd's Shop, there is no record of the Abbey board

fearing that this play might be deemed 'anti-clerical'!) A more controversial playwright was Paul Vincent Carroll. Within a period of eight years Carroll moved from the position of talented newcomer with *The Watched Pot* in 1929 to one of high esteem with *Shadow and Substance* in 1937, subsequently winning the New York Drama Critics' Circle award for the best foreign play.

Most of Carroll's works contain a dominant clerical figure. Admirers of *Shadow and Substance* somehow failed to note the sardonic bite which underscores the dialogue. Canon Skerrett is a learned but embittered priest who becomes locked in ideological conflict with a young teacher who has written a critical book on prevailing trends in Irish Catholicism. The Canon's servant girl, Brigid, an innocent who understands both men on the human level, is accidentally killed in a skirmish when a local mob seeks vengeance on the writer. Brigid may be taken as representing a confused Ireland, torn between doctrinaire and liberal values.

A number of playwrights of the 1930s provided challenging roles for women. Time has shown that Brinsley Macnamara's most considerable play is *Margaret Gillan* (1933), in which the title character's unrequited passion for the man she failed to marry, and jealousy of her daughter who ultimately marries him, is expressed with something of the same dramatic power that informs TC Murray's *Autumn Fire*. May Craig created this part with resounding success in 1933. In *Katie Roche* (1936) Teresa Deevy deals with an impetuous young woman at odds with social convention. This equally Ibsenite heroine

supplied a superb vehicle for the talents of Eileen Crowe in 1936, and thereafter for a succession of distinguished players up to the most recent production in 1994 when the part was taken by Derbhle Crotty.

Denis Johnston's first play for the Abbey, *The Moon in the Yellow River* (1931), brilliantly fulfilled his early promise at the Gate. A mocking comedy of ideas, it presents the contradictions of the Irish Free State at the point where romantic idealism and practical reality clash. The construction of a hydro-electric station in a pastoral landscape is a potent symbol for the change surrounding the birth of the nation. Of the work of the already established writers, Lennox Robinson's *Church Street* (1934) is perhaps the most interesting because of its clear indebtedness to Pirandello – an indebtedness which had already impishly surfaced in *Drama at Inish* (1933). Rutherford Mayne (*né* Sam Waddell), most of whose work was produced by the Ulster Literary Theatre, gave his best play, *Bridgehead* (1934), to the Abbey. Mildly influenced by Ibsen, it concerns the gradual disenchantment of an idealistic young man in the forestry service.

The decade ended with an imaginative scheme masterminded by Ernest Blythe for the expansion of the theatre to the adjacent riverside site, with performance spaces which would also house Dublin Gate Theatre productions and An Comhar Dramaíochta, the Irish-language drama group – a highly inclusive concept which was approved in principle by the minister for finance, delayed by an election which reduced the government majority, and abandoned on the outbreak of World War II.

FJ McCormick as Harold Mahony
and Maureen Delany as Susie Tynan
in the first production of Robinson's
The Far-Off Hills in 1928.

A later production of *The Far-Off Hills* by the Abbey Players at the Queen's Theatre in the mid-1960s proved – as with all revivals of this typically Robinsonian comedy where not everything comes right in the end – that, if ever there was an evergreen play, this is it.

opposite
Dame Ninette de Valois' 100th birthday
was celebrated with a postage stamp
in 2000. Born at Baltyboys, Co Wicklow,
she founded the Abbey School of Ballet
in 1927, having already worked with
Diaghilev. She remained as part-time
choreographer and teacher until 1933,
when the Sadler's Wells Theatre Ballet
engaged her full-time attention.

Robinson's *Church Street* (1934) was
strongly influenced by the plays of
Luigi Pirandello. The 1965 production
featured Peggy Hayes, Peadar Lamb,
Aideen O'Kelly, Desmond Cave and
Ursula Nic Lochlainn. Brenda Wilde
is at the piano.

Teresa Deevy was a prolific dramatist
of the 1940s and '50s. Though
congenitally deaf, she wrote many
successful plays for the new radio
medium. In Judy Friel's 1994
production of her most famous play,
Katie Roche, the eponymous Irish
Ibsenite heroine was played by
Derbhle Crotty.

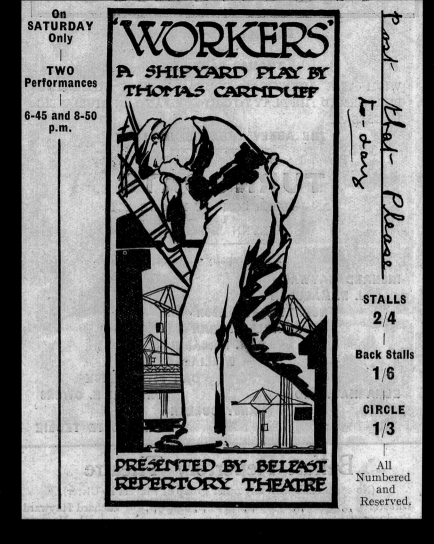

Up to the early 1930s the Abbey's own productions did not yet fill every week of the year, so the theatre was occasionally let to 'suitable' visiting companies, one of which was the Belfast Repertory Theatre. The programme for Thomas Cairnduff's *Workers* was designed by the Ulster artist Mabel Annesley.

opposite
Phyllis Ryan caused a sensation with
her playing of the innocent and saintly
Brigid in PV Carroll's *Shadow and
Substance* in 1937. She later formed her
own company, producing several plays
which had been rejected in manuscript
by the Abbey Theatre and which she
turned into international hits.

above
Tanya Moiseiwitsch, designer, and
Hugh Hunt, director, with the model
for the first production of Paul Vincent
Carroll's *Shadow and Substance* in
1937. *Shadow and Substance* won the
award for the best foreign play in New
York the following year.

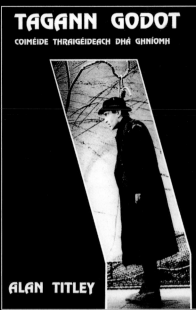

TAGANN GODOT

COIMÉIDE THRAIGÉIDEACH DHÁ GHNÍOMH

ALAN TITLEY

plays in the irish language

Opposite: The Taibhdhearc na Gallaimhe production of MacDara O Fátharta's Abbey dramatization of Máirtín O Cadhain's cryptic novel *Cré na Cille,* with the dramatist and Bríd ní Neachtain, was much praised in 1995 and 2000. *Inset:* Alan Titley's

linguistically dextrous *Tagann Godot* ('Godot Comes') won the Pater Prize for International Drama (Australia). *Above:* Antoine O Flatharta's sardonic *Imeachtaí na Saoirse* (1983), with Jonathan White, MacDara O Fátharta and Joan Sheehy.

Overleaf: Brendan Behan's *An Giall* ('The Hostage', 1958) is the only Irish-language play to be consistently performed throughout the world; the 1968 production was directed by Proinnsias MacDiarmada and designed by Brian Collins.

6

Ria Mooney as the eccentric Aunt
Hannie in Louis D'Alton's *Lovers'
Meeting* in 1941. She was the original
Rosie Redmond in *The Plough and the
Stars* in 1926, and a memorable Mary
Tyrone in O'Neill's *Long Day's Journey
into Night* in 1959.

ᵮollowing the death of Yeats at Cap Martin on 28 January 1939, 'every degrading influence from within and without was exerted on the Abbey', according to the contemporary critic Peter Kavanagh. One of the most degrading was the altering of the company's articles of association, giving powers to the board to dismiss fellow members – the targets being Frank O'Connor and the author Walter Starkie. The more reactionary members – Ernest Blythe/Earnán de Blaghad, the film censor Richard Hayes/Risteárd O hAodha, and the poet and Radio Eireann administrator Robert Farren/Roibeárd O Faracháin – were strong Irish-language revivalists, and the genuine desire within and without the theatre to provide a less marginalized forum for Gaelic drama unfortunately became associated in the public mind with a narrowing of political horizons.

The poet FR Higgins was appointed managing director shortly after the 1938 festival, but he died suddenly in 1941 with his plans largely undeveloped. His colleagues on the board unanimously requested Blythe to fill the vacancy – which he did at double Higgins' salary. George Shiels, a constant monitor of all Abbey gossip in the press, observed from his retreat in the Glens of Antrim that Blythe 'will not turn the Abbey into a highbrow clinic, but a house of intelligent entertainment'. Shiels had cause for satisfaction, for Blythe adopted Higgins' proposal for long runs rather than the traditional but more expensive one week followed by revivals when justified by initial business.

Shiels' *The Rugged Path* (1940) was the first Abbey play to achieve over 100 performances on its first run. Shiels became the most highly remunerated playwright living in Ireland. 'I am almost ashamed that my plays have monopolized the Abbey stage!' he noted. Like others in the profession, he was alarmed by reports that the theatres might close for the duration of World War II; as it turned out, the enforced absence of cross-Channel companies created opportunities for Irish managements. Attendances at the Abbey and Gate improved, and plays were produced in theatres normally devoted to opera, ballet and variety. In Belfast, Harold Goldblatt founded the Ulster Group Theatre, selecting several Abbey plays by Ulster writers such as Ervine and Shiels. The latter, however, dismissed the idea of a subsidized theatre in Northern Ireland because there was 'an absence of outstanding

• •

the full stream of national life

personalities and such a theatre could become a branch of the Civil Service'.

Ernest Blythe's twenty-six-year career as managing director did not create a civil-service ethos – his regime was more like a dictatorship. Hugh Hunt found him 'totally indifferent to criticism'; the director and designer Tomás MacAnna believed he 'ruled by force of character at once down-to-earth and commonsensical'. He possessed a highly developed sense of duty which transcended all personal feelings – in 1922 he had been a member of the cabinet that ordered the execution of four former colleagues in the Republican movement who had conspired in the murder of an elected member of Dáil Éireann.

Blythe's chief interest was the restoration of the Irish language. He wrote that the Abbey had 'slipped a little into the slack water', and believed that plays in Irish would 'bring us back into the full stream of national life'. In 1942 the state funding allocated to the independent Irish-language group An Comhar Dramaíochta was amalgamated with the Abbey's annual grant – some thought by sleight of hand. Competitions garnered some Irish scripts, but much of the work was translated from other European languages, so that when Tomás MacAnna was appointed Producer of Gaelic Plays in 1947 he had the advantage of a diversity of texts which invited a more imaginative *mise-en-scène* than was usual for the generally naturalistic plays then being produced in English.

The majority of plays in Irish were brief and were treated as afterpieces, which often resulted in a large proportion of the audience leaving their seats following the main production of the night. When Blythe instituted a Christmas entertainment in 1945 – *Muireann agus an Pionnsa*, based on Lady Gregory's wonder-play *The Golden Apple* – there was unprecedented interest, and an annual tradition was established featuring song, dance, satirical sketches, parodies of popular songs and a strong storyline usually based on Celtic mythology. This *geamaireacht* form may have lacked the polish of the corresponding English-language pantomimes at the Gaiety and Olympia in Dublin, but it succeeded in bringing in the much sought-after hoi polloi.

A perceived decline in standards of stage presentation was widely attributed to Blythe engaging players for their linguistic rather than histrionic abilities. Historians have recorded as fact that non-Irish-speaking actors were not admitted to the company, but this is no more than a myth. Nonetheless, several of the established players were in constant dread of redundancy due to an inability, or an absence of desire, to master the complexities of the language, and this did not make for a confident company. Thus another unfortunate public perception arose, to the effect that the language policy was destroying the theatre.

A much-publicized incident took place during a revival of *The Plough and the Stars* in 1947. Two young theatre enthusiasts stood up during the intermission, addressed a bemused audience, and then pointedly walked out. These were Roger McHugh, whose play *Trial at Green Street Courthouse* had been produced in 1941 and who would later become the National University's Professor of Anglo-Irish Literature, and

Valentin Iremonger, a former pupil of the School of Acting and later Ambassador to India. Iremonger berated 'the utter incompetence of the present directorate's artistic policy'. The protesters were not surprised when they received letters from members of the company agreeing with their stance.

It is clear that revivals were produced with insufficient rehearsal and inadequate cast replacements. Frank Dermody, who directed most of the new plays, was said to have been a fine teacher and theorist but weak on the practicalities of staging – Micheál MacLíammóir described him as 'a genius without talent'. After his temporary departure Ria Mooney was appointed Producer of Plays in English; she was told that 'the Abbey is at war with English', which effectively relegated half a century's repertoire to second-class status.

The success at the box office of Shiels' *The Rugged Path* disclosed public hunger for a stage image of an isolationist, neutral wartime Eire, as the country was now officially named. The play's underlying statement on the social and political demoralization of the time was not sustained in a sequel, *The Summit* (1941). Gerard Healy's *Thy Dear Father* (1943) dealt with the thorny matter of church vocations, while Seamus Byrne's *Design for a Headstone* (1950) – set in a paramilitary internment camp – aroused vocal antagonism because those with IRA sympathies believed it to be Marxist, and the Maria Duce organization saw it as yet another attack on the Roman Catholic Church. These plays may be taken to demonstrate that, in spite of its populist programme, the theatre was not neglecting serious new writing.

Among the plays of more than passing interest were St John Ervine's *Friends and Relations* (1941), BG MacCarthy's *The Whip Hand* (1942), PV Carroll's *The Wise Have Not Spoken* (1944) and Frank Carney's *The Righteous Are Bold* (1946). Joseph Tomelty, a writer associated with the Ulster Group Theatre, gave his trenchant *The End House* (1944) to the Abbey because he believed the material was too inflammatory for Belfast audiences. It deals with the effects of the Special Powers Act of 1922 on the people of a deprived urban quarter and has distinct affinities with O'Casey's plays of revolutionary Dublin.

Louis D'Alton's *The Money Doesn't Matter* (1941) and *They Got What They Wanted* (1947) are examples of the slight if well-crafted popular comedies of the period and give no suggestion that the same author was capable of more substantial stuff: his *Lovers' Meeting* (1941) deals with the constrictions on normal living imposed by Church and State, and also by the long-accepted notion of the importance of the possession of land which was ingrained in the rural psyche. The play gave Ria Mooney a superb vehicle as the crazed Aunt Hannie.

The 1940s introduced the work of a new writer from the west, Michael J Molloy, whose concerns about the erosion of indigenous culture through rural depopulation inform *Old Road* (1943) and *The Visiting House* (1946), plays in the 'poetic realism' tradition of Synge, Colum and the early Fitzmaurice. His highly popular *The King of Friday's Men* (1948), with its eighteenth-century setting, lively action and sustained eloquence, is more like one of the old-fashioned melodramas which the founders of the theatre were keen to stamp out.

● ●

overleaf left
Programme for the Abbey Experimental Theatre, a co-operative of young players and technicians which flourished from 1937 to 1950. Many participants moved on to leading roles in the Abbey, in other theatres, and in the cinema, among them Wilfred Brambell, Bill

Foley, Edward Golden, Marie Kean, Dermot Kelly, Jack McGowran, Joan O'Hara and Maureen Toal.

overleaf main image
George Shiels' bitter comedy *The Rugged Path* disclosed a raw public nerve in the first year of World War II.

It was the earliest play at the Abbey Theatre to achieve 100 performances in an initial run. This centre spread from the programme of its 100th night shows the author with his remarkably distinguished cast. The director was Frank Dermody and the designer Anne Yeats.

May Craig (Mrs. Tansey), John McDarby (Michael Tansey),
Denis O'Dea (Sean Tansey), Harry Brogan (John Perrie),
in a scene from Act One.

Mr. G

F. J. McCormick (Marcy) and Eileen Crowe (Maggie) in Act One.

Ria Mooney (
Meldon (Sergt

s—the Author.

Seumas Healy (Hugh Dolis), Cathleen Murphy (Mrs. Dolis) and James Dunne (Peter Dolis) in Act Two.

y) and Austin
e from Act One

Brid Ni Loinsigh (Miss Benny), M. J. Dolan, the Producer of the Play (Mr. Adare), and Seumas Healy (Hugh Dolis).

Trotz - 1922.

opposite
Pencil portrait of Ria Mooney (1904–73)
by Patrick Tuohy. After a career acting
and directing in Ireland, Britain and
the United States, Mooney reorganized
the Abbey Theatre School in the mid-
1930s and founded the Experimental
Theatre in 1937. In 1948 she was
appointed Producer of Plays in English.

above
The novelist and short-story writer
Frank O'Connor was a member of the
Abbey Theatre board in the late
1930s, during which time he formed
a productive relationship with Hugh
Hunt, collaborating on stage versions
of *In the Train*, *The Invincibles* and
Moses' Rock.

above
The shades of WB Yeats, Augusta
Gregory, JM Synge and Joseph
Holloway watch the burning of their
theatre. A cartoon by CE Kelly from
the August 1951 issue of *Dublin
Opinion*.

opposite above and background
After the fire, what remained of
the auditorium was used as a dump
for discarded stage properties.
The entire building was eventually
demolished to make way for the
new theatre which opened fifteen
years later.

right
As minister for finance in the first
Free State government, Ernest Blythe
(1889–1975) provided the Abbey Theatre
with an annual grant-in-aid, the earliest
such subsidy in the English-speaking
world. His greatest aim when he became
the theatre's managing director in 1941
was to create an entirely Irish-speaking
theatre, but in this he failed. He was the
driving force behind the campaign for
a new theatre following the fire of 1951.

7

Put a Beggar on Horseback, one of a series of lively comedies of Dublin life by John McCann, may be seen as typical of the fare offered while the company was resident in the Queen's Theatre from 1951 to 1966. Vincent Dowling, TP McKenna and Kathleen Barrington were among the young players recruited at this time.

On the night of 17–18 July 1951 the Abbey Theatre was accidentally destroyed by fire. The popular World War I tune 'Keep the Home Fires Burning', sung offstage in the last scene of *The Plough and the Stars,* provided an appropriate dirge for the original Abbey Theatre building's final night. The stage, workshops and most of the auditorium were burned down, but the granite frontage which contained the foyer, box office and administrative offices remained in use for several years. Almost all of the (by now) historic art collection was saved, but hundreds of playscripts were destroyed – a merciful end for some of them, it was suggested.

Members of the company gathered makeshift costumes and properties, and performed the play in the Peacock Theatre the following night to sustained applause. Ernest Blythe immediately accepted the generous offer of the newly equipped Rupert Guinness Hall from the brewing firm, and so the programme remained unbroken, with a revival of *Boyd's Shop* followed by a new play, D'Alton's whimsical comedy *The Devil a Saint Would Be.* He approached Odeon (Ireland) Ltd for a lease on the Queen's Theatre, now a down-at-heel music hall. Some perfunctory refurbishment was done to this once pretty playhouse, but not enough to render it comfortable and attractive – it was envisaged that the company would be in residence for less than five years.

The Abbey opened at the Queen's Theatre on 24 September 1951 with Ria Mooney's disastrous production of *The Silver Tassie,* a play she had directed with success at the Gaiety. Its failure was blamed on repair work that was not completed in time for proper stage rehearsals. From this inauspicious beginning a nightmare period of fifteen years ensued. It was only through the determination of Ernest Blythe to adapt to the near-impossible conditions, and to overcome the multitude of difficulties which arose with the plans for replacing the old building, that the National Theatre was saved from annihilation.

Many of the players who had formed the exemplary ensemble that had served O'Casey and a host of other playwrights so well had moved to London or Hollywood, among them Maureen Delany, Barry Fitzgerald and Arthur Shields. (A taunt in *The Bell* magazine had a curiously reasonable ring: it proposed that, as so many undistinguished plays had been made viable by these actors, it should

a grim, grey similarity

suffice for intending dramatists to omit the usual list of characters and simply indicate to which actors the roles should be allocated.) Many of the remaining permanent players felt aggrieved at being asked to take over parts for which they were unsuited, and at seeing untrained players cast in leading roles. In the week that FJ McCormick died, aged fifty-eight, exhausted and embittered, Blythe cut his salary to the non-playing rate: his wife, Eileen Crowe, made up the shortfall from her own meagre pay packet.

The 760-seat Queen's was the ideal theatre for large productions. The problem for the Abbey was that many of its plays, of their nature, could never fill such a house, and Blythe found himself accepting work which was the Irish equivalent of the light comedies of Broadway and the West End. The list of titles shows that fewer and fewer new plays of substance were performed during the company's tenure from 1951 to 1966. Eight entertaining yet eminently forgettable comedies by John McCann, from *Twenty Years a-Wooing* in 1954 to *A Jew Called Sammy* in 1962, were the hallmark of the period. Others in similar vein were D'Alton's *This Other Eden* (1953), John O'Donovan's *The Less We Are Together* (1957) and John McDonnell's *All the King's Horses* (1961).

One of the major successes was Brendan Behan's remarkable *The Quare Fellow,* in which no character speaks a line condemning capital punishment, yet the audience is left in no doubt about the author's feelings. It was produced at the Pike Theatre Club in 1954, Blythe having turned down an earlier draft, but he subsequently had the good grace to recognize its power. It is an indication of the Abbey's distancing from what was going on in Irish playwriting that the four most important plays of the time were produced elsewhere: John B Keane's *Sive* (1959) and Tom Murphy's *A Whistle in the Dark* (1961) were rejected by Blythe, and Brian Friel's *Philadelphia, Here I Come!* and Eugene McCabe's *King of the Castle* (both 1964) were not even submitted.

Certain Abbey plays, such as Carroll's *Shadow and Substance*, D'Alton's *Lovers' Meeting* and Molloy's *The Wood of the Whispering* (1953), were rediscovered by Garry Hynes' Druid Theatre Company a few decades later and shown to be much more than the conventional naturalistic dramas that they originally appeared to be. Much of the blame for absence of interpretative judgment as well as dreary staging was laid on Ria Mooney, who later wrote that her critics were unaware of the problems (presumably Blythe's lack of artistic understanding); she also bemoaned the impossibility of 'creating new settings for plays which resembled each other so closely'. This was a ludicrous situation which required an imaginative response. This was not forthcoming. Tomás MacAnna wrote: 'there was a grim, grey similarity between most of the plays which went on at the Queen's.'

As usual, there were exceptions. Walter Macken's *Home Is the Hero* (1952) is a strong play about the casting out by his family of a man returning from a lengthy term in jail; Denis Johnston's *The Scythe and the Sunset* (1958), an irreverent riposte to *The Plough and the Stars*, had a welcome air of detachment; and an unknown writer, John Murphy, contributed a charmingly wistful comedy, *The Country Boy* (1959), after which he was neither seen nor heard of again. Two early plays by Hugh Leonard, *The Big Birthday* (1956) and *A Leap in the Dark* (1957), were given, and one by Brian Friel, *The Enemy Within* (1962).

The real artistic successes at the Queen's, however, came from foreign plays. In 1959 Frank Dermody returned to direct the first Irish production of O'Neill's *Long Day's Journey into Night*; because of the lengthy run of a McCann comedy he had enough time for rehearsal and the result was a triumph, especially for Philip O'Flynn as James Tyrone and Ria Mooney as Mary. In the same year Tomás MacAnna directed Brecht's *The Life of Galileo* with Micheál O hAonghusa in a production brimming with vitality and inventiveness; and, almost as the players were vacating the Queen's, the same director gave Lorca's *Yerma* with Joan O'Hara.

When, in 1958, Archbishop McQuaid refused to celebrate a votive mass for the Dublin Theatre Festival because a new play by O'Casey was in the programme, the nervous festival committee cancelled the production, so incensing the author that he withdrew permission for *any* of his work to be performed in Ireland. The Abbey, which was not involved in the debacle, suffered most. Six years later, when the company was invited to present two of his plays in the World Theatre Season in London, O'Casey relented. By this time internal tensions had reached such a pitch that the players chose the eve of the much-publicized London visit to serve strike notice. An accumulation of grievances had been contained in a memorandum circulated by the young actor Vincent Dowling. Blythe made some concessions but refused to recognize Irish Actors Equity as a negotiating body; nor would he allow the players to use their baptismal names rather than the Gaelicized versions imposed by the management. Blythe was forced to accept a labour-court recommendation to appoint an independent arbiter; the London visit went ahead, but to a poor public response – clearly this was not the once-acclaimed company of which so much had been heard.

Blythe came under immense pressure to reform the total concept of theatre management. Dr CS Andrews, the arbiter – who had the ear of the current government – recommended salary increases in line with those of other organizations, as well as several far-reaching measures in regard to administration. As a result, a second government nominee was added to the board, and twenty-five shareholders were appointed. In turn, the new shareholders urged the government to raise the annual subsidy and to provide further funds for the completion of the long-delayed theatre building.

The shareholders also demanded the appointment of an artistic director with wide powers of play selection and casting. Ria Mooney had retired in 1963, an ill and disappointed woman; she had simply been engaged to direct whatever plays had already been chosen. Blythe resisted this development, but later conceded to the engagement of an artistic adviser in the person of the writer and director Walter Macken, who had been running An Taibhdhearc, the Gaelic theatre in Galway. As it happened, Macken was also the new government representative on the board.

"'Did you see an old woman going down the road?
... No, but I saw a young girl and she had to walk
to the Queen's.'"

above
The satirist Myles na Gopaleen (aka
novelist Flann O'Brien) waged a press
campaign for the removal of Ernest
Blythe from his post as the Abbey's
managing director during the
company's residency at the Queen's
Theatre. The sign is an abbreviated
slogan: 'Blythe must go.'

right
Cartoon from *Dublin Opinion* showing
Ernest Blythe outside the vacated old
Abbey humorously misquoting a line
from Yeats and Gregory's *Cathleen ni
Houlihan*, where the Old Woman who
represents Ireland is triumphantly
described as having 'the walk of a queen'.

opposite
Because the Queen's was much larger
than the Abbey and therefore more
difficult to fill, there were many revivals
of trustworthy plays such as Brinsley
Macnamara's 1926 comedy *Look at the
Heffernans!* Edward Golden and Joan
O'Hara appeared in the 1952 production.

opposite
The fifteen-year 'exile' at the Queen's is
wrongly remembered as a period when
there was a dearth of interesting new
plays. Denis Johnston's *The Scythe and
the Sunset* (1958) provided a sardonic
view of the Easter Rising. Doreen Madden
and Peadar Lamb played characters
wryly based on revolutionary leaders.

above
The Risen People (1958) gives an
impressionistic picture of the first
lock-out of workers by the Employers'
Federation in 1913. The author, James
Plunkett, is best known for his novel
Strumpet City. Pat Laffan, Micheál O
Bríain and Geoffrey Golden appeared
in the first production.

The gentle comedy *The Country Boy*
(1959) introduced a new writer in John
Murphy. Inexplicably, he wrote nothing
further for the theatre. Peadar Lamb
played Curley and Máire Ring was
Eileen in the first production of the
play, which remains popular after
almost half a century.

Sinéad Cusack and Donal McCann
in the name parts in *Emer agus an
Laoch,* a *geamaireacht* or seasonable
entertainment resembling the English
pantomime. For twenty years these
shows provided essential Christmas
theatregoing for non-Irish-speakers as
much as for *Gaeligeóirí.* The majority
were devised and directed by Tomás
MacAnna.

1963 publicity shot for John B Keane's *The Man from Clare,* showing the football team from a rural parish in Clare about to cross the Shannon for its first game in Kerry. Keane's earlier plays were unaccountably neglected by the Abbey Theatre.

Brian Friel's earliest play for the Abbey
Theatre, *The Enemy Within* (1962), has
at its core the missionary saint Columba's
confrontation with the nature of exile,
and its attendant private and vocational
dilemmas. Ray MacAnally was Columba,
Pat Laffan was Brian, and Micheál
O Bríain was Caornan.

european drama at the abbey

Since Lady Gregory's adaptations of Molière and Goldoni in the early years of the twentieth century, plays by European authors – Arrabal, Coppée, Euripides, Genet, Ghelderode, Ghéon, Grass, Ibsen, Sophocles, Strindberg, Valle-Inclán and others – have provided a welcome punctuation in the Abbey's programme. *Opposite, left:* In 1968 Maria Knebel came from the Moscow Art Theatre to direct Chekhov's *The Cherry Orchard* most memorably, with Siobhán McKenna as Ranyeveskaia and Cyril Cusack as Gayev. *Right:* Laurie Morton and John Olohan in Gorky's *The Lower Depths* in 1989. *Above:* Brecht's *Galileo* was directed twice by Tomás MacAnna – in his 1981

FEDERICO GARCIA LORCA's
YERMA
in a new version by
FRANK McGUINNESS

production Tom Hickey (right) played the name part, with (left–right) Geoffrey Golden and Godfrey Quigley. *Opposite, inset:* Frank McGuinness' plangent rendering of Lorca's *Yerma* was directed by Michael Attenborough in 1987. *Main picture:* In 1996 John Crowley gave a superb staging of Tom Kilroy's text from Pirandello's *Six Characters in Search of an Author,* with Andrew Scott and Gerard McSorley. *Above:* In 2000 Eamon Morrissey appeared as Don Gallant in the *Barbaric Comedies* of Ramón Maria del Valle-Inclán, in a version by Frank McGuinness.

8

Georgian houses across the street cast
their shadows on the façade of the new
Abbey Theatre, designed by Michael
Scott and Partners and opened by
President de Valéra on 18 July 1966.

a palpable improvement in spirit occurred following the opening production in the new Abbey Theatre. Morale soared within the company. Newly appointed personnel reflected a more outward-looking administration. Elections and nominations resulted in a younger board.

Ernest Blythe had succeeded where a less resolute personality would have failed. Inadequate finance, inordinately protracted delays over the purchase of adjoining properties and a succession of planning refusals and permissions were dealt with in grim sequence. Constraints such as these put an end to an imaginative plan from the architects to extend the property by one block to the riverside. An implacably plain building finally emerged containing a fan-shaped auditorium with one shallow balcony and 628 seats, a fly tower and the latest in technical equipment, and a stage that was disproportionately wide in relation to its depth. There were certain strange anomalies occasioned by paucity of consultation with heads of departments, such as absence of daylight in the wardrobe workshop and no access from it to the Peacock Theatre, which meant that costumes had to be carried out by one door, down the street and back in by another! When it finally opened on 28 July 1967, the Peacock turned out to be the major success of the project; with an end stage and raked seating for 150, it could be speedily rearranged around a central acting space, and – most unusually for a studio theatre – it possesses facilities for flying scenery.

The main auditorium was officially opened by the Irish President, Eamon de Valéra, on 18 July 1966 with a programme compiled by Walter Macken and billed as *Recall the Years*. The title alone played into the hands of the theatre's professional detractors who were waiting to pounce on any infelicity – in this case, a dull iteration of past achievements presented in a sequence of technical mishaps. After this disappointing start a run of interesting new works and several superb revivals – performed by a confident company – restored the Abbey to its central role in the hegemony of theatre in Ireland.

Walter Macken vacated his position as artistic advisor at the end of 1966 and was replaced by Tomás MacAnna. Phil O'Kelly, who brought with him experience of the intensely commercial practice of the Gaiety Theatre, was appointed as assistant to Ernest Blythe. When Blythe retired in 1967, O'Kelly became manager, Blythe remaining on the board for five more years. An immensely important innovation, largely

• •

two new theatres

necessitated by the doubling of the annual number of productions due to year-round operation in the Peacock, was the engagement of new directors, whether as staff or on limited contracts – Sean Cotter, Vincent Dowling, Roland Jaquarello, Pat Laffan – or as guests – Michael Cacoyannis, William Chappell, Tyrone Guthrie, Eugene Lion, Colm O Bríain, Jim Sheridan, Max Stafford-Clark and Voytek – as well as successive artistic advisors or artistic directors. This created a much greater range of styles and approaches than had ever been witnessed before.

One of the more curious trends of the time was the unusual number of dramatizations of other literary forms. The two outstanding successes in the years immediately following the opening of the new theatres were PJ O'Connor's enormously entertaining version of Patrick Kavangh's autobiographical novel *Tarry Flynn* (1966), with Donal McCann as the rustic poet and Máire ní Dhomnaill as his garrulous mother, and Frank McMahon's *Borstal Boy* (1967), taken from Brendan Behan's autobiography, with Niall Tóibín and Frank Grimes as the older and younger Behan. Between 1968 and 1971 there were adaptations from Eric Cross, James Joyce, Flann O'Brien, Frank O'Connor, Peadar O Laoghaire and Pádraig O Síochfhradha. The most frequently revived would be Eric Cross's racy memoir *The Tailor and Anstey*, which gave a suberb vehicle to the actor Eamon Kelly as the idiosyncratic tailor of the title and led to Kelly's remarkable sequence of one-person shows recalling the rural past.

This period would still have been remarkable if nothing had been produced but four new plays by Tom Murphy. His epic *Famine* (1968) looked at this harrowing subject beyond the particularities of Ireland in the 1840s. This was followed by *A Crucial Week in the Life of a Grocer's Assistant* (1969), a candid comedy of small-minded small-town life in a totally different mode. Its particularization of the poverty of mind which drives the young from Ireland was a change for an audience accustomed to the gentle provincial satires of Lennox Robinson. *The Morning after Optimism*, Murphy's threnody on innocence and experience, appeared two years later. In a chimerical forest redolent of *amour courtois* literature or tapestry, a romantic young couple encounter a raddled and embittered ponce and whore – an image of what they will become. Reality intrudes abrasively into the dream. Bryan Murray and Nuala Hayes were the innocents, and Eithne Dunne and Colin Blakeley the destructive older couple, in a production by Hugh Hunt that was distinguished by Bronwen Casson's luminescent décor.

Idealism and disillusion, emigration and return, are themes constantly explored and intertwined in Murphy's work. In 1972 Vincent Dowling directed *The White House*, with Dan O'Herlihy as JJ Kilkelly, a provincial publican and John F Kennedy lookalike who so idolizes the 'returned emigrant' President that he assumes his persona. When Kennedy is assassinated JJ's self-esteem, and his stature as a local quasi-hero, are instantly demolished. The sham of Ireland's claim to the glory of the Kennedy charisma is exposed.

Eugene McCabe, a major dramatist whose early work passed the Abbey by, provided the theatre with the script of his *Swift* in 1969; the theatre then provided McCabe with Tyrone Guthrie as director and Micheál MacLíammóir as leading actor, and this unlikely mingling of capricious talents almost upset the balance of this vivid reflection on a great mind's decline into madness. In 1973 the theatre commissioned a play from Brian Friel, whose work with other managements had by now established him as a leading dramatist in Ireland and abroad. This resulted in *The Freedom of the City* (1974), written as a response to the Bloody Sunday massacre in Derry the previous year. Sometimes categorized as 'documentary drama', it is far too profound in its analysis of outrage, too complex in its construction, too amusing (given the circumstances) on the shibboleths of Orange and Green, to be so conventionally labelled.

From the opening of the new theatres in 1966 to the resignation of Lelia Doolan as artistic director in 1972 there was a sequence of five artistic advisors/directors – six if Tomás MacAnna's second term is counted. Successive boards have been blamed for appointing unsuitable candidates, and then for antagonizing their choices. Certainly some of the appointees were simply unable to cope with the unexpected complexities of internal politics, involving not only the board but the powerful Players' Council and the Staff Council. Hugh Hunt, invited to replace Alan Simpson (the founder of the innovative Pike Theatre, who stayed at the Abbey for less than a year), later wrote that he insisted the term 'artistic director' be used 'since it was essential that the post carried with it the full duties of an executive officer rather than an adviser'. Hunt considered his appointment to be of an interim nature

until an Irish theatrical personality were found. This personality turned out to be Lelia Doolan, but she, in turn, felt it necessary to relinquish the post after a year and a half. Hindsight suggests that those who at some time earlier in their careers had been a part of the Abbey were most likely to succeed, while 'outsiders' generally failed.

The litany of appointments and resignations engaged the attention of the press as much as did the programme of plays. There were several hugely successful productions from outside the usual field. One was Boucicault's *The Shaughran*, presented in a bewitching panorama of painted scenes by Alan Barlow, with performances by Cyril Cusack and Donal McCann that transcended the merely comic; another was the first Abbey production of a major Beckett play, Sean Cotter's *Waiting for Godot* with Donal McCann and Peter O'Toole; yet another was Chekhov's *The Cherry Orchard*, directed by Maria Knebel from the Moscow Art Theatre with Cyril Cusack and Siobhán McKenna. The company now made up for few or poor appearances abroad with *The Shaughran* in London, *She Stoops to Conquer* in Paris, *The Hostage* in five European cities, *The Shadow of a Gunman* in Florence and Tomás MacAnna's Tony award-winning *Borstal Boy* in New York. *The Silver Tassie* was given in Brussels to mark Ireland's entry to the European Economic Community. O'Casey would certainly have relished this second apotheosis; what he might have thought of the new Roman Catholic Archbishop of Dublin attending a performance is quite imponderable.

The stalls of the new theatre, with
a set by Frank Conway for *The Plough
and the Stars.*

Recall the Years by Walter Macken
was the opening production in the
new theatre. A compilation of
reminiscences and memorable moments
from famous Abbey plays, it signalled
an obsession with the past which
depressed many theatregoers and
members of the profession.

Frank McMahon's adaptation of
Brendan Behan's autobiographical
Borstal Boy, directed by Tomás
MacAnna, was a major success in 1987
and later on Broadway where it won
the Tony Award for best new play.

The famous wake scene from Dion
Boucicault's *The Shaughran* directed
by Hugh Hunt and designed by Alan
Barlow in 1975, 100 years after its first
Dublin production at the Theatre Royal.
This kind of play was anathema to
Yeats and Lady Gregory.

Niall Toibín appeared to hilarious
effect in Wesley Burrowes' surreal
comedy *The Becauseway*, which won
for the author the Irish Life Drama
Award in 1970. Best known for his
television drama, Burrowes has
contributed significantly to the
liberalizing social debate in Ireland.

Eugene McCabe's major plays were produced elsewhere until 1969, when Tyrone Guthrie was engaged to direct *Swift*, with Tanya Moiseiwitsch returning as designer. Micheál MacLíammóir (left), seen here with Geoffrey Golden, was guest *artiste*. It was said that these strong personalities caused almost as much drama offstage as on.

overleaf left
Cyril Cusack as Conn the Shaughran, a photographic study by Dermot Barry.

overleaf right
Tom Murphy's caustic fable *The Morning after Optimism* was brilliantly served in its first production in 1971 by its director Hugh Hunt, designer Bronwen Casson, and actors Colin Blakeley and Eithne Dunne.

opposite
Angela Newman, Eamonn Morrissey and
Raymond Hardie in *The Freedom of the
City* (1973). Set in Derry at the time of the
Bloody Sunday massacre, it is Brian Friel's
only play occasioned by a specific event.
It is strongly satirical of both Unionist
and Nationalist tribal mythologies.

Hatchet, Heno Magee's violent play of
contemporary life in a deprived quarter
of Dublin, was first produced in 1978.
The cast was made up of leading
players of the time: Máire Hastings,
Desmond Perry, Geoffrey Golden, Anita
Reeves, John Kavanagh, Mauren Toal,
Michael Duffy and Colm Meaney.

• •

american plays at the abbey

With the exception of plays by Eugene O'Neill, American drama was sparse on the Abbey stage until the second half of the twentieth century. Since then, Henley, Mamet, McClure, Miller, Shepard, Wilder, Williams and others have all been produced. *Opposite:* Patrick Mason directed Kushner's *Angels in America* in 1995, with Jonathan Arun as Prior Walter. *Above:* Tom Hickey and Liam Neeson appeared in Steinbeck's *Of Mice and Men* in 1980. *Overleaf, left:* Joe Dowling's production of Kaufman and Hart's *You Can't Take it with You* proved irresistible in 1995. *Right:* Brian Dennehy (left) in Garry Hynes' production of *The Iceman Cometh* in 1989.

9

For over twenty years Eamon Kelly
provided a series of rich characterizations
in his solo performances recalling the
customs and sayings of an almost forgotten
rural past. He also played leading roles in
countless plays, among them PJ O'Connor's
dramatization of *The Tailor and Anstey* by
Eric Cross, in which he was the Tailor.

following the resignation of Lelia Doolan in 1973, Tomás MacAnna took up the post of artistic director (formerly 'adviser') for the third time. The actor and director Vincent Dowling, who would become the company's artistic director fourteen years later, wrote of Doolan that she possessed 'the vitality, the vision, the artistic and educational experience… but she did not have the support of the Abbey. Curious coalitions brought her down.' MacAnna belonged: he had complete comprehension of every faction within the Abbey, a knowledge of every corner and crevice of the institution.

By now the concept of industrial democracy was becoming accepted in both the public and private sectors. At the Abbey, the Players' Council and the Staff Council were each allotted a seat on the board. The apparatus of state funding also changed: from 1976 the department of finance ceased to provide direct subvention, this function being passed to the Arts Council. Thus the National Theatre Society now found itself at a remove from the fountainhead, dependent upon the availabilty of funds from a body which in turn had to convince the department of the needs of its numerous clients. There was the curious anomaly of the minister for finance continuing to nominate two members to the theatre's board, while the Arts Council made do with a non-voting observer.

The perspective of time has shown that at no period in the Abbey's history was so much attempted as in the 1970s. The greatest change was in the number of non-Irish plays presented, as if the Abbey were taking on the work of other companies. While the objective of encouraging and presenting new Irish plays remained central, the founders would have been astonished by the diversity of the material: musicals, revues and pantomimes became almost as much a routine component as 'legitimate' drama. This inclusion of more non-Irish work may have been resented by purists who subscribed to Yeats and Gregory's rather grudging notion of a limited complement of 'dramatic works by foreign authors', but it was welcomed by theatregoers, and more especially by members of the acting company to whom it afforded a much greater range of roles – in 1974, for example, there were productions of Antrobus, Arrabal, Brecht, Chekhov, Ibsen, Lorca, Storey, Strindberg, Molière and Tennessee Williams. This internationalist programme seems to have arisen for pragmatic reasons rather than as a result of any deeply debated policy. There was the need to keep two theatres going for

a wider world

fifty-two weeks of the year, the desire of directors and designers to extend their range, and the wish to attract distinguished visiting artistes.

The most immediately visible vehicle for change, however, was the new and well-equipped Peacock Theatre. Its sense of intimacy encouraged a style of playing comparable to that which had existed in the old Abbey. It was also ideally suited to productions of plays which were not expected to draw large crowds, and to 'experimental' plays. The Peacock also became the home of Irish-language drama.

During the new Abbey's first ten years there were twenty-one Irish-language productions, nineteen of which were staged in the Peacock. A considerable range, from folk drama to rock opera, was exemplified in the work of Padraig O Giollagáin, with *An Choinneal* (1967), *Fleadh* (1972) and *Johnny Orfeo* (1973). *Fleadh* – the word signifies a public merrymaking with music and dance – draws on a bacchanalian tradition in Gaelic poetry and storytelling which (surprisingly) has not often been made use of in the theatre; here, a man who has been wrongly diagnosed as terminally ill decides to live every remaining moment of his life to the full, with hilarious and touching results.

An outstanding bilingual author, Criostóir O Floinn, contributed several works. *Mise Raiftéirí an File* (1973) treats of the dilemma of the blind Antoine O Raiftérí (1784–1835), who travelled from house to house making poems at the time when his native language was rapidly disappearing. O Floinn considers questions of cultural decline in a highly theatrical fashion, anachronistically introducing figures of the Literary Revival such as Lady Gregory and Douglas Hyde to heighten the sense

of loss as well as the late rediscovery of Gaelic culture and its absorption into the new literature.

Mairéad ní Ghráda was probably the most consistently provocative Irish-language playwright. Her *Breithiúnas* ('Judgment', 1968) considers the nation's achievement of forty years through the eyes of a dying politician, and finds its fictional hero – and the new Irish state – wanting in probity. The critic Robert Welch has compared the plays of certain modern Gaelic dramatists favourably with those of their English-language contemporaries Brian Friel, Thomas Kilroy and Tom Murphy, in respect of the significance of themes explored, and their stature as dramatic art. The shame is that the work has reached such a small public.

In Murphy's intensely disturbing *The Sanctuary Lamp* (1975) three derelicts of society share the pain and disappointment of their lives in a church where the sustaining presence of a loving God is vengefully absent. Friel contributed *Volunteers* to the Abbey stage in the same year; the men of the title are political prisoners working on an architectural dig – they are likely to be executed by fellow internees on account of their co-operation with the authorities. Excavation of the past provides a multifaceted metaphor, and the author's developing engagement with language as both an instrument and a barrier to communication is brought forward, later to be made spellbindingly manifest in *Translations*. In Friel's *Living Quarters* (1977) an Irish army officer returns, Theseus-like, from foreign service, expecting the laurel crown, but finds his family life so besmirching that he has no option but suicide.

In 1976 came Max Stafford-Clark's chiaroscuro production of Thomas Kilroy's *Tea and Sex and*

Shakespeare. Ernest Blythe had rejected Kilroy's trenchant and humane *The Death and Resurrection of Mr Roche* eight years earlier; this play became the hit of the Dublin Theatre festival of 1968, and – with the attitude that usually accompanies changes of personnel – was later produced twice at the Abbey. The Abbey staged Kilroy's *The O'Neill* at the Peacock in 1969, but the acceptance of *Tea and Sex and Shakespeare* disclosed a new willingness to attempt work that was both thematically and formally challenging. The following year Patrick Mason directed Kilroy's *Talbot's Box* on the Peacock stage. Matt Talbot was a familiar street figure in Dublin in the early twentieth century, a docker and reformed alcoholic who took upon himself the sins of humanity through acts of kindness and mortification of the flesh. An object of some hilarity to the worldly-wise, he was revered by the pious and was accorded Venerable status by the Vatican. Kilroy's brilliantly conceived and executed play deals with the nature of genuine holiness and charity in the face of greed and injustice. His kaleidoscopic collage of literary and colloquial speech forms make a poignant contrast with the perceived inarticulacy of the man himself.

Other outstanding plays of the period were Hugh Leonard's surreal *Time Was* (1976) and Stewart Parker's *Catchpenny Twist* (1977), the latter one of many examples of the work of playwrights from Northern Ireland finding a readier welcome in Dublin than at home.

Since settling in England in the late 1920s, Sean O'Casey had written a number of plays in the waning expressionist mode that promoted a mildly Marxist agenda. They received scant attention in Ireland until Tomás MacAnna produced *Purple Dust*, *Cock-a-Doodle Dandy* and *The Star Turns Red* at the Abbey in the 1970s. George Shiels had written that O'Casey's later plays were 'noisy and pretentious, and most of the argument unreal and elementary', but Shiels failed to grasp that they can succeed as directors' and designers' pieces.

The Peacock Theatre was a superb space for the plays of Yeats – the old Peacock had the intimacy, but not the technical facilities. *Purgatory* and *The Herne's Egg* were given in 1973, and in 1978 two plays in the Noh manner, *At the Hawk's Well* and *The Only Jealousy of Emer*, were staged by the Japanese director Hideo Kanze. Samuel Beckett's *Happy Days*, with a touchingly dotty Marie Kean as Winnie, was directed by Jim Sheridan in 1973 in the Peacock: it was only the company's third encounter with the work of the émigré Dublin writer, from whom, inexplicably, neither the Abbey nor any other Irish theatre commissioned work.

Occasional productions of Shakespeare had been seen at the old Abbey. In 1975 a young company member, Joe Dowling, used the considerable resources of the Peacock and a highly motivated group of recently recruited players to present an entrancing *Twelfth Night*, designed by Bronwen Casson. The following year *Much Ado about Nothing* was given in the same manner, and a year later *Measure for Measure*, directed by Pat Laffan. Many of the actors were part of the vibrant 'Young Abbey' which toured to schools but became the victim of a serious budgetary crisis in 1974 after only four years. In 1975 Dowling joined the Irish Theatre Company (the national touring ensemble) as artistic director. When Tomás MacAnna relinquished the Abbey's artistic directorship in 1978, Dowling was appointed to succeed him.

May Cluskey played a succession of
brilliant character roles in the 1970s
and '80s. Her one-person show *Mothers*
was repeated many times after its
first performance in 1976.

Niall O'Brien as Smiler and Bryan
Murray as Desmond in the first
production of Brian Friel's *Volunteers*,
directed by Robert Gillespie in
1975. The volunteer archaeologists
unearth 'a tangible précis of the
story of Irish man' over 1,000 years.

In 1974 there was a definitive new
production of Lennox Robinson's
timeless comedy from 1916, *The
Whiteheaded Boy*, directed by Tomás
MacAnna and designed by Brian
Collins. Bryan Murray (seated centre)
played the title role, with Deirdre
Donnelly, Veronica Duffy, Aideen
O'Kelly, Máire O'Neill, Clive Geraghty
and Eileen Colgan.

Patrick Mason directed the first
production of Thomas Kilroy's *Talbot's
Box* in 1977. John Molloy played
the masochistic Catholic mystic of the
Dublin slums. Eileen Colgan and
others sustained a multiplicity of roles
in this laceratingly entertaining and
touching work.

Jim Sheridan directed the first
production of Tom Murphy's *The Blue
Macushla* in Chicago gangster-land
motion-picture style in 1980. Among
the cast were Fedelma Cullen, Donal
McCann, Emmet Bergin, Peadar Lamb,
Pat Leavy, Deirdre Donelly, Paddy Long
and Stephen Rea. The designer was
Brian Collins.

above
Wendy Shea's setting for Eugene
O'Neill's *Desire under the Elms* in 1976.

opposite
Lorcan Cranitch as Robert Gibson and
Joan O'Hara as his mother in Sebastian
Barry's *The Only True History of Lizzie
Finn* (1995). A love story encompassed
by intricacies of nationality, class and
culture, it was directed by Patrick Mason
with costumes by Joan O'Clery and set
design by Joe Vanek.

Yeats' Noh-inspired play of 1917 *At the
Hawk's Well* at the Kauze Nogakudo,
Tokyo, in 1990. The Old Man was played
by Shiraishi Kayoto, the Young Man by
Tomoeda Teruyo and the Guardian of the
Well by Asami Masakuni. The photograph
was taken by Yoshikoshi Tatsuo.

Ingrid Craigie, Karen Ardiff and
Catherine Walsh in Hugh Leonard's *Love
in the Title*, in which three women with
contrasting lives in different time zones
engage in a dialogue that illuminates
their varied experiences. It was directed
by Patrick Mason and designed by Joe
Vanek in 1999.

Clockwise from top left
Brian Friel by Basil Blackshaw; Hugh
Leonard by Robert Ballagh; Tom Murphy
by Carey Clark (all in the Abbey Theatre
Collection); Frank McGuinness by Paul
Funge (in the Dublin Gate Theatre
Collection).

opposite
Thomas Kilroy's *The Secret Fall of
Constance Wilde* was directed by Patrick
Mason in 1997, with movement directed
by David Bolger and design by Joe
Vanek. Jane Brennan played Constance.
Disturbing relationships are projected
with a fertile sense of theatricality.

overleaf
Frank McGuinness's *Observe the Sons
of Ulster Marching towards the Somme*
was first produced in 1985, revived later
the same year, and given in a new
production in 1995. Directed by Patrick
Mason on each occasion, this 1995
production was designed by Joe Vanek.
It has appeared in other productions
around the world.

10

Poster by Brendan Foreman for the
first production of William Trevor's
Scenes from an Album, directed by Joe
Dowling in 1981.

Joe Dowling's term as artistic director from 1979 to 1985 was characterized by an expanded company, an unprecedented flowering of new writing talent and the annexation of several vanguard Irish plays which had previously been deployed outside the Abbey Theatre. The ever-evolving board was now chaired by Micheál O hAodha, an author and Radio Eireann drama producer. Joe Dowling had grown up within the Abbey and was therefore accepted by the long-established players and staff. By the time of his appointment the new Abbey and Peacock stages had been tested with every imaginable kind of drama, entertainment and spectacle. It was time to make a serious appraisal of the Abbey's *raison d'être*: Irish playwriting.

Even during the dramaturgically sterile Queen's Theatre period, as many as 300 scripts a year were received from hopeful authors: how many potentially animated works had been extinguished by the haphazard selection system? In 1974 the shareholders recommended that the board engage an experienced playwright to oversee the receipt and return of unsolicited work and propose the production of those which seemed viable. In turn, Denis Johnston, Hugh Leonard and Thomas Kilroy held this part-time position; perforce, their own

writing commitments took precedence. Kilroy advised the board that the post should be full-time and include editorial responsibility. In 1979 Sean McCarthy was appointed as script editor. Writers of discernible promise now received the kind of guidance which had been missing since the time of Lady Gregory, and workshops of seemingly intractable material often led to successful productions. Among the playwrights who emerged in the Dowling–McCarthy era were Neil Donnelly, Bernard Farrell, Frank McGuinness, Antoine O Flatharta and Graham Reid. At the same time established writers such as Brian Friel, John B Keane, Hugh Leonard, Tom MacIntyre and Tom Murphy seemed to enter a phase of greater involvement with the Abbey, however much their work was presented by managements elsewhere.

While work by these authors was in train the company continued to present the kind of eclectic programming introduced by Tomás MacAnna, which resembled that of the recently established National Theatre of Great Britain. Stoppard's *Night and Day* and Miller's *All my Sons* exemplify the breadth of choice. There were productions of *A Midsummer Night's Dream* and *The Merchant of Venice*, and Michael Bogdanov directed Stephen Brennan in a *Hamlet* set

● ●

theatrical aristocrats

in a corrupt present-day dictatorship. Dowling's penchant for farcical comedy was seen at its most accomplished in Goldoni's *The Servant of Two Masters*, Kaufman and Hart's *The Man Who Came to Dinner* and Feydeau's *Hotel Casanova* in a saucy version by Fergus Linehan. Fergus and Rosaleen Linehan adapted James Stephens' wry, socially conscious novella of 1923 *The Charwoman's Daughter* as a musical, *Mary Makebelieve*.

Bernard Farrell's first play *I Do Not Like Thee, Dr Fell* (1979), takes place during a twenty-four-hour session of an encounter group where one of those present, the sceptical Joe Fell, questions the honesty of the organizer and his fellow participants, who seem unable to accept the truth about themselves. The play struck an instantaneous chord with audiences in Paul Brennan's production and has become the author's most performed play throughout the world. *Canaries*, a comedy of delusion, followed in 1980; *All in Favour Said 'No!'* (1981) targets trades-union custom and practice; *All the Way Back* (1985) is a comedy of domestic concealment.

Graham Reid's first play, *The Death of Humpty Dumpty* (1979), deals with the appalling side effects of sectarian violence in Belfast. A caring husband and parent accidentally witnesses a shooting and is subsequently shot by the perpetrators at his own front door; permanently disabled, he becomes a monster. The desperately animated head on the virtually dead body is an unforgettably horrific stage image of Northern Ireland during the euphemistically termed 'Troubles'. Neil Donnelly is as caustic an observer of the moral brutalities of contemporary life in the Republic as is Reid of the more overtly politicized

northern society. His first play, *Upstarts* (1980), was followed by *The Silver Dollar Boys* (1981), in which the narrow religious-dominated educational system is seen as training schoolboys for a life that drifts in the direction of crime. Antoine O Flatharta's *Gaeligeoirí* appeared in the same year; it deals with the relative hopelessness of the scheme for inculcating schoolchildren with a knowledge of the Irish language in the broader context of the breakdown of the social system of the Gaeltacht districts.

By far the most inspirational new play produced during the artistic directorship of Joe Dowling was *Observe the Sons of Ulster Marching towards the Somme* (1985) by Frank McGuinness. McGuinness had already contributed *Factory Girls* (1982), remarkable as a first piece for its depth of characterization and natural buoyancy of dialogue. As is often the case with revolutionary works of art, few of those involved in the first production seemed to anticipate its power to move the audience, and most critics attending the early performances failed to note a crucial event in Irish playwriting where one Ireland spontaneously recognizes another.

Observe the Sons of Ulster is the product of an extraordinary fusion of objectivity (research) and the subjective impulse (intuition). In his final hours, the one-time iconoclast Kenneth Pyper is attended by the shades of former comrades who served in the almost entirely Protestant 36th Ulster Division in northern France in 1916; their loyalty to faith, to friends, to the minutiae of local lore and landscape – to Ulster – is recalled amid intimations of the destruction of their very culture. Emotion is recollected in horror, horseplay and affection. Pungent colloquial speech (with a distinct flavouring of the King James Bible) is a binding force.

Friel's *Aristocrats* and Leonard's *A Life* were both directed by Dowling in 1979. In *Aristocrats* John Kavanagh added to his lengthening list of superbly realized character roles as the deluded Casimir O'Donnell, heir to a disintegrating family and ancestral house. In *A Life*, Cyril Cusack and a splendid company of experienced players demonstrated that the Abbey ensemble was as richly endowed and ready to entertain as it had ever been, in this comedy of quintessential bourgeois yearnings and deceits.

Tom Murphy's *The Blue Macushla* (1980) received such elaborate staging that the material all but vanished in the *mise-en-scène*. His *The Gigli Concert* (1983) is a work of mythic proportion and operatic intensity. It was sparingly directed by Patrick Mason, with Godfrey Quigley and Tom Hickey as opposite extremes of the same obsessive neurosis. The writer Colm Toibín described the play as using Ireland 'as a backdrop, an Ireland of corruption and loss of faith, but it allowed its voice to soar above the actual'.

The poet and novelist Tom MacIntyre had had several plays presented at the Abbey and elsewhere before his collaborative engagement in 1983 with the director Patrick Mason and actor Tom Hickey on *The Great Hunger*, inspired by Patrick Kavanagh's anti-epic poem. It was intended that the physicality of staging would release the drama from the tyranny of the spoken text: yet it would have been impossible to repress entirely MacIntyre's at once supremely gnomic, allusive and joyous use of language.

These new works apart, undoubtedly the most significant development was the gathering into the Abbey fold of a number of major Irish plays of the past twenty-five years which had initially been produced elsewhere. In 1981 Dowling obtained Friel's *Faith Healer,* which had been spectacularly unsuccessful in New York, and revealed it on the Abbey stage with Donal McCann, Kate Flynn and John Kavanagh as the author's finest work to date. In 1982 he directed *Philadelphia, Here I Come!,* which had been Friel's earliest international success. In 1983, only three years after its premiere with the Derry-based Field Day Theatre Company, Dowling acquired Friel's *Translations.* Similarly, Dowling added Hugh Leonard's *Da* (first produced in the United States), a perennially poignant comedy of the father–son relationship, to the Abbey repertoire. Looking back much further to 1959 when the Abbey had famously spurned John B Keane's *Sive*, this drama of primordial passions at last reached the Abbey stage in 1985, when it became the first in a succession of reappraisals of Keane's work.

Sive, with its savage exposure of the ritualistic sacrifice of a young woman, is far from being the stereotypical 'rural drama'. Like Friel's *Philadelphia* and *Translations*, the locale is distinctly familiar, but the implication is global, and the technique of presentation is nothing if not adventurous. Plays such as these had burst out of the straitjacket of 'peasant' – or at least 'domestic' – realism; what audiences were now offered was the familiar cottage kitchen or village pub as a disguise for something more potent, or as a starting point for a drama of much wider resonance in relation to Irish history, customs and myth.

overleaf
During Sean McCarthy's script editorship, an unusual number of new writers were introduced, among them Bernard Farrell. His *I Do Not Like Thee, Dr Fell* (1979) was directed by Paul Brennan, with John Molloy, Billie Morton, Garrett Keogh (as Joe Fell), Kathleen Barrington, Paul Murphy, Fiona MacAnna and Tom Hickey.

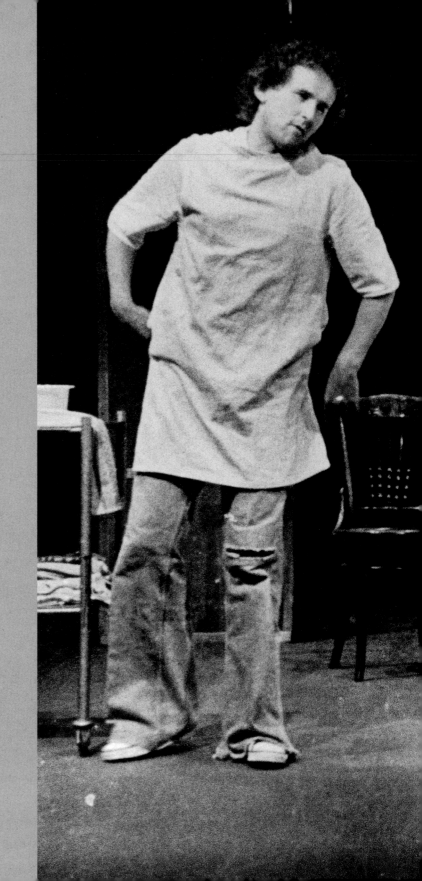

Graham Reid's pungent play about
the effects of the 'Troubles' on non-
participants, *The Death of Humpty
Dumpty*, was directed by Patrick
Mason in 1979, with Colm Meaney,
Clive Geraghty and Liam Neeson.

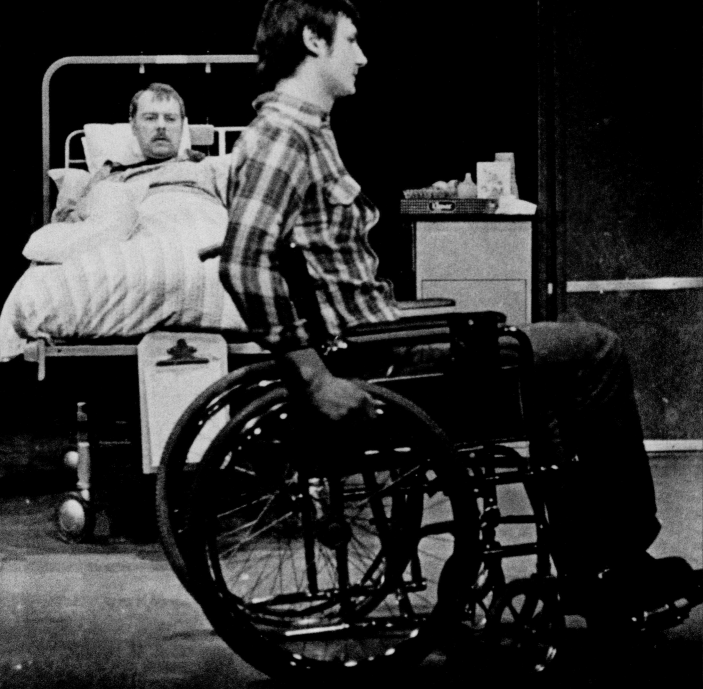

Kate Flynn and Colm Meaney in
Stewart Parker's *Nightshade*, directed
by Chris Parr and designed by Bronwen
Casson in 1981. Like Ervine and Shiels
before them, Reid, Parker and other
playwrights from Northern Ireland
found a readier market for their work
in Dublin than Belfast.

Ulick O'Connor's documentary play *Executions* was first directed by Tomás MacAnna in 1985 and published by the Brandon Press. A later rehearsed reading directed by Patrick Mason in the room where the fateful decisions were made by the first Free State government created an extraordinarily uncanny atmosphere.

Neil Donnelly's *The Silver Dollar Boys* in 1981 followed his success with *Upstarts* in the previous year. Directed by Ben Barnes, *The Silver Dollar Boys* was revived in 1982 and again in 1986. Tom Hickey is seen here as the reactionary Brother Duffy, the Irish-language teacher.

Tom MacIntrye is one of Ireland's most prolific playwrights, cerebral yet instinctual, combining ancient memories with contemporary confusions. An intensely physical *mise-en-scène* is essential. Most Abbey productions have been collaborations with the director Patrick Mason and the actor Tom Hickey. Above: Conal Kearney, Tom Hickey and

Fiona MacAnna appeared in the first production of *The Great Hunger* (1983, designed by Bronwen Casson). Opposite: in *Good Evening, Mr Collins* (1995, directed by Kathy McArdle; designed by Barbara Bradshaw) Bríain F O'Byrne played the revolutionary leader and Karen Ardiff the three women who sustained him.

abbey plays in overseas
productions

Dozens of plays that originated on the Abbey stage have been produced in other countries, whether in English or Irish or translated into European, African or Asiatic languages. *Opposite, left:* Sean O'Casey's *Juno and the Paycock* enjoyed one of its reincarnations at the Ermolova Theatre in Moscow with E Kirollova and V Razinkova. *Right:* Joe Dowling's 1997 production of JM Synge's *The Playboy of the Western World* at the Guthrie Theater in Minneapolis, USA, with Derdriu Ring, Caitlin O'Connell and Michael Hayden. *Above, left:* Denis Johnston's *The Moon in the Yellow River* appeared at the National Theatre of Poland in Warsaw in 1936, only five years after its Abbey production. *Right:* Brian Friel's *Dancing at Lughnasa* was directed by Hiroko Watanabe for the Min-gei company in Tokyo in 1993 in a replica of the original Abbey set.

11

Brenda Fricker and Johnny Murphy in
Ben Barnes' production of John B Keane's
1967 play *Big Maggie* in 1988. Joe Dowling,
as artistic director, initiated several new
productions of plays that had originally
been produced, thus reinvigorating
and absorbing important works into the
National Theatre repertoire.

Joe Dowling resigned his position as artistic director in the spring of 1985 following what were described in the press as 'differences of opinion with the board'. During no other period since the early years of the century had such a luscious cluster of new plays been produced, and never had there been such consistent technical excellence.

First-rate standards were achieved at a cost: there was now a very large resident company, and expenditure – chiefly on salaries – rose above income to an alarming degree. Dowling believed that high production values could not be maintained with considerably fewer personnel. Undoubtedly there was pressure from the board on that cliché prescription for dissension between governors and artistic administrators, artistic freedom. Meetings under the chairmanship of Charles McCarthy became less than conciliatory, if occasionally alleviated by philosophical digressions on such arcane topics as the nature of the Abbey style of acting. Dowling moved to the Gaiety Theatre, where he produced a successful range of popular classics which undoubtedly damaged the Abbey box office. He was subsequently appointed director of the celebrated Guthrie Theater in Minneapolis.

Tomás MacAnna, still a member of the board, was temporarily re-entrusted with the company's artistic affairs, reducing the financial deficit somewhat. The current author, Christopher Fitz-Simon (who had succeeded Sean McCarthy as script editor in 1983), was promoted to the post of artistic director in 1986. In spite of the gradual implementation of the board's decision to reduce staff, and a scheme of voluntary redundancy for players, the financial position worsened, due partly to extravagant productions of Flann O'Brien's *The Hard Life* and Farquhar's *The Beaux' Stratagem*, and partly to an uninspired programme at the Peacock.

Certainly the situation was not helped by unusually damaging press comment. Dowling was popular with the media and no opportunity was spared to draw the public's attention to the unhappiness which now existed within the institution. The loss to the Gate of Frank McGuinness's *Innocence* was a severe blow. The death of three much-admired actors in the early months of 1986 spread the pall of despondency.

An upturn in the financial position was registered in the summer of 1986 with two Irish plays which had not yet been seen at the Abbey: Hugh Leonard's comedy

● ●

ministry of all the talents

The Patrick Pearse Motel, Feydeauesque in form but rather more mordant than that *boulevardier* would ever have essayed; and Tom Murphy's groundbreaking *A Whistle in the Dark* with Garry Hynes, founder of the Druid Theatre Company in Galway, as guest director. These coincided with a revival of Tom MacIntyre's *The Great Hunger*, which proceeded to the Edinburgh Festival and thence to London and Paris, considerably brightening the company's image.

The general perception that the Abbey was once again in terminal decline was also offset by Frank McGuinness's *Bag Lady* (1985), a monologue of distress and loss performed with consummate emotional and technical virtuosity by Maureen Toal; the same author's plangent version of Lorca's *Yerma* (1987); and his *Carthaginians* (1988), in which a group of women reminiscent of those in *Factory Girls* are united in a vigil of hope in which the trauma of Bloody Sunday in Derry – and indeed the entire experience of the 'Troubles' – may be purged.

While the core Abbey company was in process of disintegration a number of actors who had come to prominence in the younger companies such as Druid, Rough Magic and Red Kettle were engaged, among them Anne Byrne, Darragh Kelly, Pauline McLynn, Maoliosa Stafford and Michael Murphy, introducing a much-needed breath of fresh air. Early in 1987 a new production of John B Keane's *The Field*, with Niall Toibín as Bull McCabe, drew enormous crowds, as did Bernard Farrell's new comedy, *Say Cheese*, with David Kelly as Valentine Fagan; both were directed by Ben Barnes. As a result, by the end of the year there was a small operating surplus, but not enough to reduce the cumulative deficit appreciably.

At this time the new chairman, Professor Augustine Martin, was searching for an internationally respected theatrical figure to take up the artistic directorship in the long term. Thus it was that Vincent Dowling, director of the Cleveland Playhouse and formerly a highly active member of the Abbey company, rejoined the organization in the early summer of 1987. In the event he stayed for only two years, while maintaining his connection for a third as fundraiser and promoter for the Abbey in the United States. The financial constraints imposed by the long-standing deficit curtailed his plans. Disappointingly, his vision for the company seemed to be for the Abbey as it had existed twenty years before. He organized a lengthy and highly successful American tour of *The Playboy of the Western World* with Frank McCusker as the Playboy.

Arresting new plays, however, continued to appear. Michael Harding's cryptic *Strawboys* (1987) introduced a new talent which was to develop with *Una Pooka* (1990), a play of fractured perceptions disclosing a society viscerally at odds with itself. The poet and novelist Sebastian Barry's first play, *Boss Grady's Boys* (1989), showed exceptional promise – a promise splendidly fulfilled the following year with the deeply sensitive *Prayers of Sherkin*, in which a nineteenth-century nonconformist English sect, in numerical decline on an island off West Cork, brings illumination to the people of the mainland; both plays were atmospherically directed by Caroline Fitzgerald. Tom Murphy's *Too Late for Logic* (1989), a saturnine comedy of private and public disenchantment, brought a sharp contemporaneity to the programme, while Neil Donnelly's equally topical *The Reel McCoy* (1989), in which government and civil-service corruption is frighteningly projected, somehow failed to make the impact it deserved.

In 1989 the board appointed one of its own members, the impresario Noel Pearson, to the post of artistic director, recognizing that the kind of experience he could provide was essential in both programme and fiscal undertakings. A long-term representation to government in respect of the cumulative deficit finally resulted in an *ex gratia* payment of £400,000.

Surprisingly, Brian Friel offered his new play, *Dancing at Lughnasa* (1990), to the Abbey rather than to his own Field Day Theatre Company. While other factors contributed, the revitalization of the company may be seen as starting with this production. *Dancing at Lughnasa,* for all its presentiment of the breaking up of the rural social order in the 1930s, produces an effect in the theatre – like *Observe the Sons of Ulster* – of something at the very heart of life, of the victory of human resilience and love over the tyrannies of fate. The production was revived many times during the ensuing decade; it also played in London and New York, where it gathered a cornucopia of awards, and at one time two Abbey casts were performing it simultaneously in different corners of the world.

In January 1991 Noel Pearson returned to the commercial theatre, having passed the artistic directorship to Garry Hynes. She was the sixth artistic director in eight years – a succession recalling the appointments, resignations and dismissals of the 1930s and 1970s. In 1991, Marina Carr's *Ullaloo,* which had been awaiting production for some time and revealed a highly original talent waiting to be released from Beckettian thrall, Antoine O Flatharta's *Silverlands* (in English) and Sean MacMathúna's *A Winter Thief* (performed in English and Irish) signalled another expansion of the range of new writing. Two supremely confident social comedies by masters of the craft were Hugh Leonard's cross-generational fantasy *Moving* (1992) and Bernard Farrell's corrosive *The Last Apache Reunion* (1993), in which the past of a group of former schoolmates is uncomfortably revealed.

A novel interpretation of *The Plough and the Stars* irritated traditionalists unable to understand that the theatre is ephemeral but the text eternal. A salutary project was the presentation in 1993 of three plays by Billy Roche collectively titled *The Wexford Trilogy.* The first had been turned down some years before largely due to the company's weariness with plays of Irish provincial angst set in the past, no matter how well written, and a view that the modern public would give short shrift to such work. These plays were acclaimed in Britain, where they were regarded as novel. Garry Hynes subsequently commissioned Roche's *The Cavalcaders* (1993), a play in the same vein of love unrequited and promise unfulfilled, with an affecting musical element.

Garry Hynes' term ended in a year of real consolidation of resources, with plays from Brian Friel (*Wonderful Tennessee*), Michael Harding (*Hubert Murray's Widow*) and Gerry Stembridge (*Ceausescu's Ear*), and the introduction of a new playwright in Jimmy Murphy.

Una Pooka (1989), Michael Harding's
second play for the Abbey Theatre,
is about homicide and impersonation
in a country that seems recognizable but
recedes disturbingly into stranger and
more menacing territories. Sean
McGinley, Barry McGovern and Gabrielle
Reidy were directed by Patrick Mason
in a design by Monica Frawley.

Des Nealon, Liam Carney, Johnny Murphy and Eanna MacLiam in *Brothers of the Brush* (1993), a comedy of trades-union and workplace malpractice by Jimmy Murphy. Directed by David Byrne and designed by Paul McCauley, it introduced a vibrant new writer whose work rapidly developed in the theatre and broadcasting.

STRIKE ON HERE

STRIKE ON HERE

In Brian Friel's *Dancing at Lughnasa*
(1990), the story of the disintegration of
a rural family in the 1930s Free State is
told in elegiac language. As directed by
Patrick Mason and designed by Joe Vanek,
it found an immediate response wherever
the Abbey Theatre performed it around
the world. The cast in 2000 included Anna
Healy, Anita Reeves and Lynn Cahill.

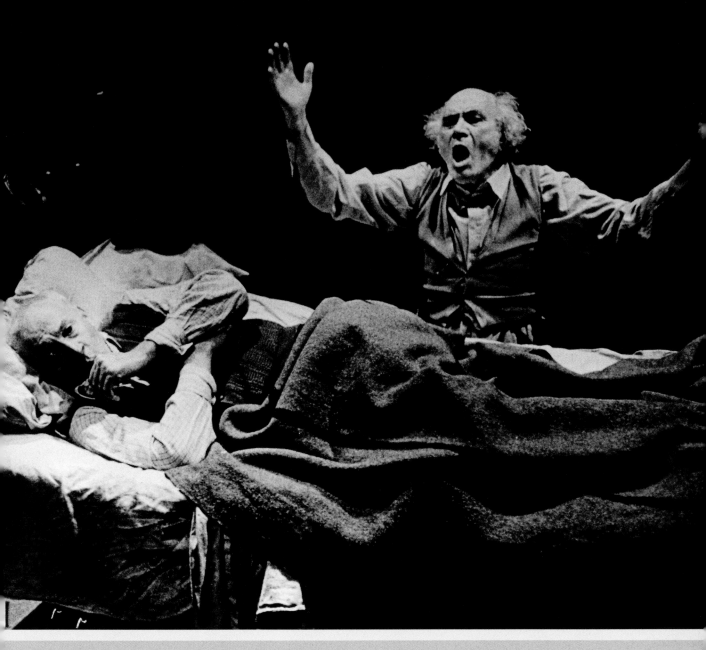

Already established as an innovative
writer of prose fiction, Sebastian
Barry's first play for the Abbey was
Boss Grady's Boys (1989). Jim Norton
and Eamon Kelly gave extraordinarily
touching performances as the
bachelor brothers. Direction was
by Caroline Fitzgerald and design
by Carol Betera.

Brendan Kennelly's version of *The Trojan Women* equates the suffering, resilience and determination of Euripides' women with those of the Ireland of his time. It was sumptuously staged by Lynne Parker, with set and costumes by Frank Conway. Birdie Sweeney played Poseidon and Helene Montague was Pallas Athena.

Billy Roche's muted comedies of lost
illusions in provincial townscapes failed
to interest the Abbey until they had been
well received elsewhere. Garry Hynes
subsequently brought these plays to the
Peacock Theatre and also commissioned
The Cavalcaders (1993), with the author,
Tony Doyle and Barry Barnes in the cast.

12

Des Nealon dreams in Niall Williams'
A Little Like Paradise (1995). The
sublime world of the spirit is never far
from the confident regularities of
village life. Brian Brady directed and
Jamie Vartan designed this wistful
morality tale by an internationally
acclaimed author.

When Patrick Mason accepted the post of artistic director in 1994 he had directed over fifty productions with the company, collaborating on many of the most innovative and prestigious manifestations of the Abbey Theatre's enduring presence. Among these were Thomas Kilroy's *Talbot's Box*, Tom Murphy's *The Gigli Concert*, Frank McGuinness's *Observer the Sons of Ulster Marching towards the Somme*, Brian Friel's *Dancing at Lughnasa* and a remarkable sequence of plays by Tom MacIntyre. He brought with him a high degree of creativity coupled with a strong sense of professional discipline. The institution benefited enormously from the coincidence of his appointment with the chairmanship of the lawyer James Hickey and their declared intention of speaking with one voice: too often in the past board and artistic management had been heard to differ.

Between 1994 and 1995 the Abbey published three policy documents representing the most complete exposition of the history, philosophy and daily operation of any theatre in Ireland. A response was sought to these from the Arts Council, but such answer as there was tended to confirm the view that the Council had lost its way in relation to the professional theatre, preferring the uninformed and transitory to the substantial and lasting. A series of open meetings designed to broaden the theatre's relationship with the public was organized in 1994; unluckily, it coincided with a programme of neglected masterpieces from the repertoire which failed to attract the audience, causing a temporary financial crisis.

During Patrick Mason's six years as artistic director there were startlingly powerful productions of Irish and foreign plays. Without doubt Synge's *The Well of the Saints* had never been so commandingly realized. Ben Barnes brought fresh insights to O'Casey's *Juno and the Paycock* in a manner that was authoritative rather than meddlesome. There was Tony Kushner's sensational *Angels in America*, a vivid new version by Conall Morrison of Kavanagh's *Tarry Flynn*, and Jane Brennan as Shaw's *St Joan*. A succession of new plays underpinned the policy that had been evolved 100 years before: Lady Gregory's admonition to writers to be 'critical of life' was as clearly heard as ever.

'What can I do but enumerate old themes?' Yeats had enquired in a late mood of self-deprecation; yet old themes regalvanize themselves in new contexts, using – in the theatre – novel techniques of staging.

• •

all art is a collaboration

The perennially vexing matter of Irish identity was explored by Neil Donnelly in *The Duty Master* (1995), set surprisingly among the cricketing classes of the English shires. In *Give Me Your Answer, Do!* (1997) Brian Friel again addressed the problem of the creative artist, this time in terms of the scale of values placed on a writer's work by the outside world as well as by the writer himself. The endemic self-mutilation of working-class Ulster Protestantism was violently revisited by Gary Mitchell in *In a Little World of our Own* (1997) and *As The Beast Sleeps* (1998), plays which were given scant attention in their native province. The lot of the underprivileged in a state which had painfully experienced emigration but not immigration was taken a step further in Donal O'Kelly's trenchant *Asylum! Asylum!* (1994). In Jimmy Murphy's *A Picture of Paradise* (1997) and *The Muesli Belt* (2000) the specifics of personal dislocation in an all too rapidly changing environment provided a welcome renovation of the Dublin urban drama.

Niall Williams' *A Little Like Paradise*, Sebastian Barry's *The Only True History of Lizzie Finn* and Dermot Bolger's *April Bright* – all appearing serendipitously in 1995 – may be seen as the work of authors skilled in other forms of literature making evocative use of the stage in a non-realistic fashion. Williams' play dealt with rural decline and rebirth in a manner as far removed from a social tract as any sensitive poet might wish; Barry, by means of a love story set at the time of the Anglo–Boer wars, disclosed a suppressed page from the story of modern Ireland's formative years; and Bolger supplied the past of a forgotten community through the medium of a suburban house that vibrates with memories, peopled by those who may be seen as 'the detritus of history'.

While several of Sebastian Barry's past-haunted plays were first presented by other managements, most of Marina Carr's first productions during the 1990s were at the Abbey. The sequence of *The Mai* (1994, directed by Brian Brady), *Portia Coughlan* (1996, directed by Garry Hynes) and *By the Bog of Cats* (1998, directed by Partick Mason) is characterized by recklessly unhappy personal relationships in a newly evolved provincial society that is only one generation removed from peasant or itinerant culture; the language is scabrous, intensely local in idiom and syntax. As with many of the younger Irish dramatists, much use is made of the searching monologue through which the desperation in the speaker's soul finds its expression.

Taking a physical incident in its heroine's life as its starting point, Thomas Kilroy's *The Secret Fall of Constance Wilde* (1997) has only three speaking characters – Oscar Wilde, his lover, Lord Alfred Douglas, and his wife; an androgynous figure, six masked attendants and an immense and terrifying father-figure puppet fill out the drama of mendacity and the search for personal salvation, set at a time when Ireland was escaping from one tyranny and entering another. Patrick Mason's direction, David Bolger's movement direction and Joe Vanek's design rose superbly to the physical as well as the emotional challenge of the work.

Patrick Mason introduced the posts of archivist and voice coach, and formally agreed an association with the School of Drama at the Samuel Beckett Centre in Trinity College (Dublin University), an arrangement that had been considered over a long period but resisted at board level. An energetic outreach programme was initiated. In 2000 Ben Barnes – who also had a distinguished history as a director with the company – was appointed to follow Mason. In 2002 Eithne Healy was elected to the chair. Martin Fahy, the long-standing general manager who had weathered countless fiscal and operational storms, retired with honour in the same year.

With increased activities, difficulties arising from the inadequacy of the theatre plant became more acute. Stores and workshops had long ago moved out to inconvenient suburbs. In 1995, with financial help from the Guinness Trust, a plan for complete rebuilding on the existing site was drawn up, but the government was slow to commit funds and a further delay was occasioned by a proposal to relocate to an immediately available dockland site a mile downstream. In 2003 the government agreed to support a 100 million-euro scheme to be partly financed from the private sector, in which the theatre would expand over adjoining properties. The tardiness of the decision meant that plans for a building worthy of the National Theatre would only be at the discussion stage at the time of the company's centenary celebrations.

Almost all of the great plays of the Irish theatre since 1904 originated in the Abbey Theatre, and most of those that did not were later absorbed into its repertoire. A hundred years hence the social commentator will understand the preoccupations, the inconsistencies, the haunting obsessions of Irish life far better from the content of the plays than from any political or demographic studies, for the plays encompass the ethos of their time. Delegates at conferences of the world's national theatres never fail to marvel at the ability of Ireland's National Theatre to maintain an arresting programme that is free of artificially induced material – and representatives of the national theatres of countries of comparably small population are envious of the continuing production of new works, their repertoires being largely composed of established plays borrowed from other cultures,

Half a century ago Micheál MacLíammóir – who, as a founder of the Dublin Gate Theatre, might have been seen as one of the Abbey's chief rivals – wrote that 'however many and bitter the problems that beset Irish life, there is in Ireland a vigorous body of intellect that has boldly coped with these problems… and while the Abbey Theatre stands these problems will find their way to the light in the form of plays'. His words echoed those of William Butler Yeats and Lady Gregory fifty years earlier when they had arrogantly asserted that they would show the world that in Ireland there existed 'that freedom of expression without which no new movement in art or literature can succeed'. As long as these conditions persist, and as long as its inquisitive and demanding audience remains, the Abbey Theatre will continue to provoke, amuse and astonish the theatregoing world.

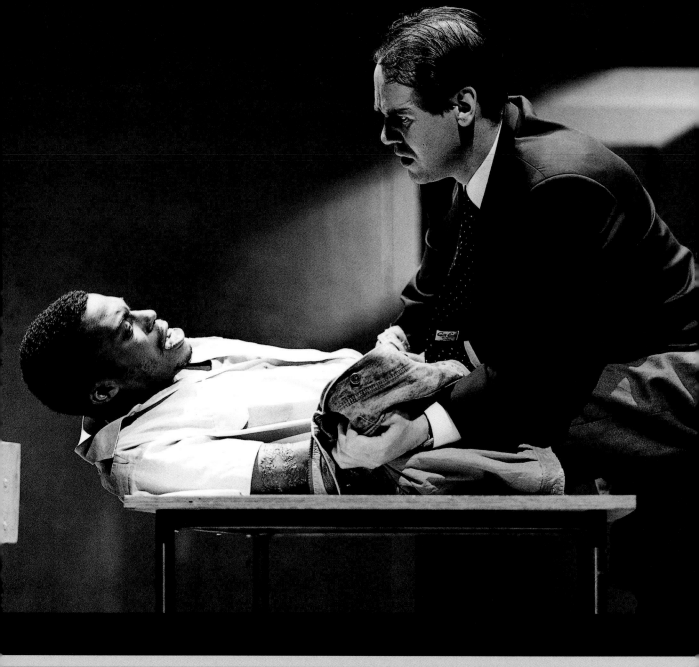

Dave Fishley played the African migrant
Joseph Omara and David Herlihy was the
immigration officer Leo Gaughran in
Asylum! Asylum!, Donal O'Kelly's
trenchant play about repressive and
inhumane Irish immigration laws. The
author is also a much-admired actor.
John Crowley directed in 1994, and the
designer was Paul McCauley.

Dermot Crowley, Mario Rosenstock and
Michael Devaney in Neil Donnell's *The
Duty Master* (1995). The Irish past of
a teacher at an English public school is
as irritatingly pervasive as his present
is socially muddled and his future
unnervingly unsure. Ben Barnes directed
and Joe Vanek designed this pithy play.

Dermot Bolger's *April Bright* (1995).
David Byrne's delicately realized
production was designed by Monica
Frawley, with Máire ní Ghráinne,
Dawn Bradfield, Eithne Woodcock
and Fedelma Cullen. The author explores
family feelings in a house where
a daughter is terminally ill. The house
itself plays an influential role.

Patrick Kavanagh's *roman à clef Tarry Flynn* (1948) was adapted for the stage by PJ O'Connor in 1966 and again in this new version of operatic sweep and vivacity by Conall Morrison in 1997. Design was by Francis O'Connor and the hayseed hero was played by James Kennedy.

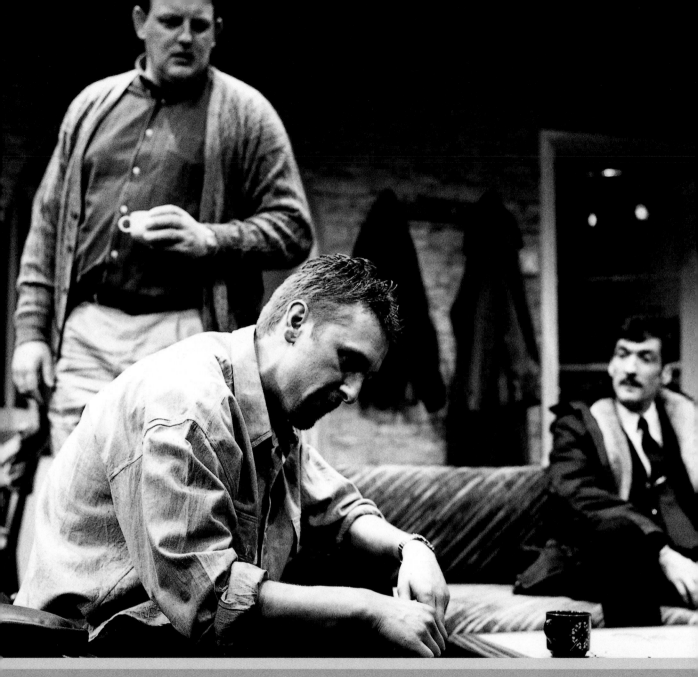

Internecine violence in a Protestant
working-class suburb of Belfast informs
Gary Mitchell's *In a Little World of our
Own*. Directed by Conall Morrison and
designed by Kathy Strachan, this was
the author's earliest play to be staged by
the Abbey Theatre. Sean Kearns,
Stewart Graham and Lalor Roddy
played leading parts.

Joan O'Hara as Grandma Fraochlain and Derbhle Crotty as Millie in Marina Carr's *The Mai* (1994), directed by Brian Brady and designed by Kathy Strachan. 'Marina Carr takes the chronicle mode and studies it, plays with it,' says Tom MacIntyre. 'Chronicle and pictorial fuse… She is a quest-writer. She puts her life on the line.'

overleaf left
Aideen O'Kelly and David Kelly in Brian Friel's own production of his *Give Me Your Answer, Do!* (1997). The play tackles questions of how writing is valued, not valued or undervalued; the value writers place upon themselves; and the doubt that smoulders in the heart of the creative artist.

overleaf right
Marion O'Dwyer and Barbara Brennan in Bernard Farrell's sixteenth play, *Kevin's Bed* (1999), directed by Ben Barnes with set design by Frank Hallinan Flood and costume design by Joan O'Clery. Memory plays tricks; the unexpected revelation convulses the participants, and laughter rocks the theatre.

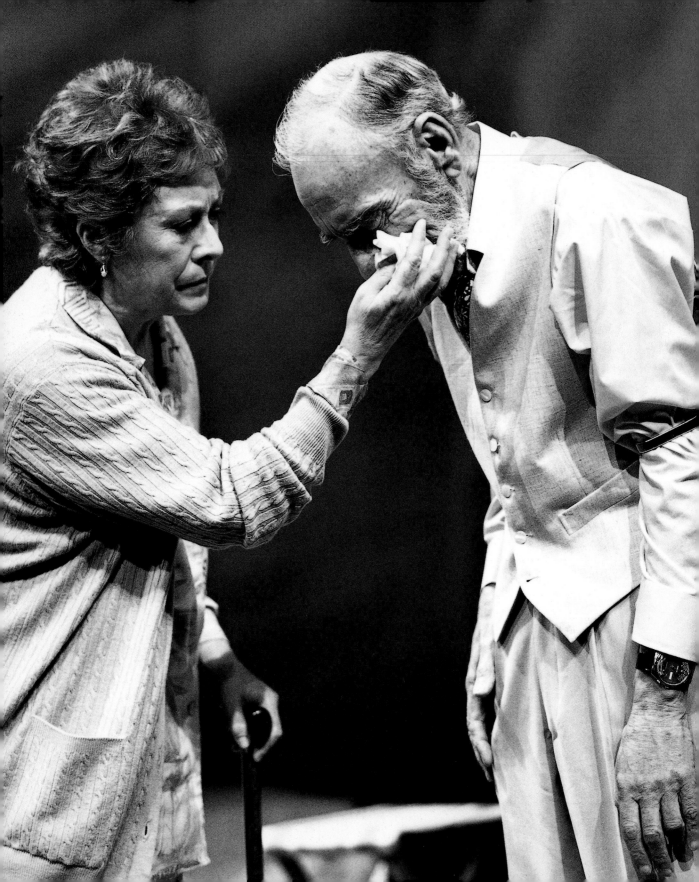

Conor McDermottroe as Carthage
Kilbride, Pauline Flanagan as Mrs
Kilbride, Siobhán Cullen as Josie
Kilbride and Pat Leavy as Monica
Murray in Marina Carr's *By the Bog
of Cats,* directed by Patrick Mason
and designed by Monica Frawley in
1998. Euripidean terror is encompassed
by pitiless laughter.

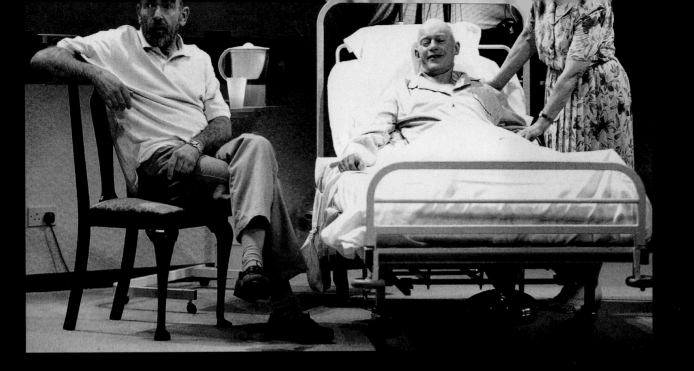

Bosco Hogan as Arthur McLoughlin,
Peter Hanly as Jordan McHenry and
Stella McCusker as Martha McHenry
in *Communion* (2002) by Aidan Mathews,
a play of deep emotional feeling
expressed in luminescent colloquial
language. The director was Martin Drury
and the designer Francis O'Connor.

overleaf left
John Kavanagh as the much
misunderstood Mr Drumm in Ben
Barnes' production of Hugh Leonard's
A Life in 2000. The same actor played
the same character in Patrick Mason's
production of Leonard's *Da* in 2002.

overleaf right
Ingrid Craigie as Frances and Mark
Lambert as Fermoy in Marina Carr's
Ariel, directed by Conall Morrison
in 2002 with costume design by Joan
O'Clery and set design by Frank Conway.

Fiona Shaw as Medea in Deborah
Warner's production in 2000.

Garry Hynes, founder of the Druid
Theatre Company, directed many plays
at the Abbey Theatre before and after
her 1991–93 artistic directorship.

Marina Carr, six of whose plays, as well
as a collaboration, were presented by the
Abbey Theatre between 1991 and 2003.

De Blaghd, Earnán: *Trasna na Bóinne.* Dublin, 1957

Clarke, Brenna Katz, and Ferrar, Harold: *The Dublin Drama League.* Dublin, 1979

Costello, Peter: *The Heart Grown Brutal.* Dublin, 1977

Dowling, Vincent: *Astride the Moon.* Dublin, 2000

Ellis-Fermor, Una: *The Irish Dramatic Movement.* London, 1939

Fallon, Gabriel: *The Abbey and the Actor.* Dublin, 1969

Fay, Gerard: *Cradle of Genius.* Dublin, 1958

Fay, WG, and Carswell, C: *The Fays of the Abbey Theatre,* London, 1935

Fitz-Simon, Christopher: *The Boys.* London, 1994

Gregory, Augusta: *Our Irish Theatre.* London, 1913

Gregory, Augusta: *Lady Gregory's Journals* (2 vols). Gerrard's Cross, 1978, 1987

Grene, Nicholas: *The Politics of Irish Drama.* Cambridge, 1999

Hogan, Robert: *After the Irish Renaissance.* Minneapolis, 1967

Hogan, Robert, Kilroy, James, and others: *The Modern Irish Drama* (6 vols). Dublin, Newark and Gerrard's Cross, 1976–1992

Holloway, J (ed. Hogan and O'Neill): *Impressions of a Dublin Theatregoer.* Carbondale, 1967

Hunt, Hugh: *The Abbey: Ireland's National Theatre.* Dublin, 1979

Kavanagh, Peter: *The Story of the Abbey Theatre.* Orono, 1976

Kiberd, Declan: *Inventing Ireland.* London, 1995

MacAnna, Tomás: *Fallaing Aonghusa: Saol Amharclainne.* Dublin, 2001

McCann, Seán: *The Story of the Abbey Theatre.* London, 1967

Mercier, Vivian: *Modern Irish Literature.* Oxford, 1994.

Mikhail, EH: *The Abbey Theatre.* London, 1988

Mooney, Ria: *Players and the Painted Stage.* Newark, 1978

Moore, George: *Hail and Farewell* (3 vols). London, 1911–13

Murray, Christopher: *20th-Century Irish Drama.* Manchester, 1997

Nic Shiubhlaigh, Máire, and Kenny, Edward: *The Splendid Years.* Dublin, 1955

O'Connor, Frank: *My Father's Son.* Dublin, 1968

O'Connor, Ulick: *Celtic Dawn.* London, 1984

O Siadhail, Pádraig: *Stáir Drámaíochta na Gaelige.* Indreabháin, 1993

O'Neill, Michael: *The Abbey at the Queen's.* Nepean, 1999

Robinson, Lennox: *The Irish Theatre.* London, 1939

———: *Ireland's Abbey Theatre.* London, 1941

Roche, Anthony: *Contemporary Irish Drama.* Dublin, 1994

Ryan, Phyllis: *The Company I Kept.* Dublin, 1996

Trewin, JC: *Benson and the Bensonians.* London, 1960

Watt, Stephen (ed.): *A Century of Irish Drama.* Bloomington, 2001

Welch, Robert: *The Abbey Theatre 1899–1999.* Oxford, 1999

Yeats, WB: *Autobiographies.* London, 1955

Pauline Flanagan as Mommo in Tom Murphy's own production of his 1985 play *Bailegangaire*, presented during the Abbey Theatre's celebration of six of his plays in 2001.

essential reading

This is a chronological list of the plays presented in the last century by the National Theatre Society at the Abbey and Peacock Theatres, Dublin. A considerable number of the plays given below have been performed there many times throughout the century, either as revivals or in new productions: the following is a list of their first appearances. Titles in heavy type are those of original plays; other titles are of first productions at the Abbey or Peacock Theatres of already existing Irish plays, as well as international classics and the work of foreign dramatists.

1904
Padraic Colum: *Broken Soil**
Augusta Gregory: *Spreading the News; Twenty-Five**
Seamus McManus: *The Townland of Tamney**
JM Synge: *In the Shadow of the Glen*; Riders to the Sea**
WB Yeats: *On Baile's Strand; The Hour Glass*; The King's Threshold*; The Shadowy Waters**
(* Given by the National Theatre Society at other venues prior to the opening of the Abbey Theatre)

1905
William Boyle: *The Building Fund*
Padraic Colum: *The Land*
Augusta Gregory: *Kincora; The White Cockade*
JM Synge: *The Well of the Saints*

1906
William Boyle: *The Eloquent Dempsey; The Mineral Workers*
Augusta Gregory: *Hyacinth Halvey; The Gaol Gate; The Canavans*
WB Yeats: *Deirdre*
Augusta Gregory: *The Doctor in Spite of Himself* (from Molière)

1907
Wilfred Scawen Blunt: *Fand*

George Fitzmaurice: *The Country Dressmaker*
Augusta Gregory: *The Jackdaw; The Rising of the Moon; Dervorgilla*
Douglas Hyde and Lady Gregory: *The Poorhouse*
WM Letts: *The Eyes of the Blind*
JM Synge: *The Playboy of the Western World*
WB Yeats and Lady Gregory: *The Unicorn from the Stars*
Maurice Maeterlinck: *Interiors*

1908
WF Casey: *The Man Who Missed the Tide; The Suburban Groove*
George Fitzmaurice: *The Pie-Dish*
Augusta Gregory: The Workhouse Ward
Thomas MacDonagh: *When the Dawn has Come*
Conal O'Riordan: *The Piper*
Lennox Robinson: *The Clancy Name*
WB Yeats: *The Golden Helmet*
Augusta Gregory: *Teja* (from Sudermann); *The Rogueries of Scapin* (from Molière)
Richard Brinsley Sheridan: *The Scheming Lieutenant*

1909
Edward Dunsany: *The Glittering Gate*
Augusta Gregory: *The Image*
DL Kelleher: *Stephen Gray*
WM Letts: *The Challenge*
RJ Ray: *The White Feather*
George Bernard Shaw: *The Shewing-Up of Blanco Posnet*
Conal O'Riordan: *An Imaginary Conversation*
Lennox Robinson: *The Cross Roads*
Augusta Gregory: *The Miser* (from Molière)

1910
Padraic Colum: *Thomas Muskerry*
Augusta Gregory: *The Travelling Man; The Full Moon; Coats*
TC Murray: *Birthright*
RJ Ray: *The Casting-Out of Martin Whelan*
Lennox Robinson: *Harvest*
JM Synge: *Deirdre of the Sorrows*

WB Yeats: *The Green Helmet*
Augusta Gregory: *Mirandolina* (from Goldoni)

1911
Edward Dunsany: *King Argimenes and the Unknown Warrior*
St John Ervine: *Mixed Marriage*
Augusta Gregory: *The Deliverer*
Douglas Hyde: *A Nativity Play* (tr. Augusta Gregory)
Anon: *The Interlude of Youth; The Second Shepherd's Play*
Douglas Hyde: *The Marriage* (tr. Augusta Gregory)
Rutherford Mayne: *Red Turf*
WB Yeats: *The Land of Heart's Desire*

1912
William Boyle: *Family Failing*
Joseph Campbell: *Judgment*
St John Ervine: *The Magnanimous Lover*
Augusta Gregory: *MacDonough's Wife; Damer's Gold; The Bogie Man**
EH Moore: *A Little Christmas Miracle*
TC Murray: *Maurice Harte**
Lennox Robinson: *Patriots*
Anon: *Annunciation; The Flight into Egypt; The Worlde and the Chylde*
Douglas Hyde: *An Tincéir agus an t-Sidheóg*
WB Yeats: *The Countess Cathleen*
(* Given by the National Theatre Society at the Royal Court Theatre, London, prior to performance on the Abbey stage)

1913
Joseph Connolly: *The Mine Land*
SR Day and GD Cummins: *Broken Faith*
St John Ervine: *The Critics*
George Fitzmaurice: *The Magic Glasses*
John Guinan: *The Cuckoo's Nest*
Mrs Bart Kennedy: *My Lord*
TC Murray: *Sovereign Love*
Seumas O'Kelly: *The Bribe*
Seamus O'Brien: *Duty*
GS Paternoster: *The Dean of St Patrick's*

first productions 1904—2003

RJ Ray: *The Gombeen Man*
Gertrude Robbins: *The Homecoming*
Rabindranath Tagore: *The Post Office*
Gerhardt Hauptmann: *Hannele*
August Strindberg: *There Are Crimes and Crimes; The Stronger*

1914
RA Christie: *The Dark Hour*
St John Ervine: *The Orangeman*
F Jay: *The Cobweb*
JB McCarthy: *Kinship; The Supplanter**
MJ McHugh: *A Minute's Wait*
Edward McNulty: *The Lord Mayor*
Con O'Leary: *The Crossing*
VO'D Power: *David Mahony*
Walter Riddall: *The Prodigal*
WP Ryan: *The Jug of Sorrow*
AP Wilson: *The Cobbler; The Slough*
Richard Brinsley Sheridan: *The Critic*
(* Given by the National Theatre Society at
the Royal Court Theatre, London, prior to
performance on the Abbey stage)

1915
William Crone: *The Bargain*
St John Ervine: *John Ferguson*
Augusta Gregory: *Shanwalla*
MJ McHugh: *The Philosopher*
FC Moore and WP Flanagan: *By Word
of Mouth*
Lennox Robinson: *The Dreamers*

1916
William Boyle: *Nic*
Bernard Duffy: *Fraternity; The Coiner; The
Counter Charm*
John Guinan: *The Plough Lifters*
DC Maher: *Partition*
Lennox Robinson: *The Whiteheaded Boy*
George Bernard Shaw: *John Bull's Other
Island; Arms and the Man; Widowers' Houses*

1917
St John Gogarty with Joseph O'Connor:
Blight
John Barnewall: *The Bacach*
SR Day and GD Cummings: *Fox and Geese*
Herbert Farjeon: *Friends*
JB McCarthy: *The Crusaders*
MJ McHugh: *Tommy-Tom-Tom*
Seumas O'Kelly: *The Parnellite*
RJ Purcell: *The Spoiling of Wilson*
RJ Ray: *The Strong Hand*
George Bernard Shaw: *Man and Superman;
The Inca of Perusalem; The Doctor's
Dilemma*

1918
EF Barrett: *The Grabber*
Christian Callister: *A Little Bit of Youth*
Maurice Dalton: *Sable and Gold*
WR Fearon and Roy Nesbitt: *When Love
Came over the Hills*
Augusta Gregory: *Hanrahan's Oath*
Dorothy Macardle: *Atonement*
Rose McKenna: *Aliens*
TC Murray: *Spring*
Lennox Robinson: *The Lost Leader*

1919
Sadie Casey: *Brady*
Padraic Colum: *The Fiddler's House*
Daniel Corkery: *The Labour Leader*
Edward Dunsany: *A Night at an Inn*
Desmond Fitzgerald: *The Saint*
Augusta Gregory: *The Dragon*
Brinsley Macnamara: *Rebellion in
Ballycullen*
Seumas O'Kelly: *Meadowsweet*
Con O'Leary: *Queer Ones*
Gideon Ousley: *A Serious Thing; The
Enchanted Trousers*
WB Yeats: *The Player Queen*
George Bernard Shaw: *Androcles and the Lion*

1920
F Barrington: *The Deaman in the House*
Daniel Corkery: *The Yellow Bittern*
St John Ervine: *The Island of Saints*
Augusta Gregory: *The Golden Apple*
Brinsley Macnamara: *The Land for the
People*
Stephen Morgan: *The Serf*
FJH O'Donnell: *The Drifters*
Fergus O'Nolan: *A Royal Alliance*
KF Purdon: *Candle and Crib*
James Stephens: *The Wooing of Jane
Elizabeth*
Edward Dunsany: *The Tents of the Arabs*
Oliver Goldsmith: *The Good-Natur'd Man*
George Bernard Shaw: *The Devil's Disciple*

1921
Bernard Duffy: *The Piper of Tavran*
Augusta Gregory: *Aristotle's Bellows*
Terence MacSwiney: *The Revolutionist*
Edward McNulty: *The Courting of
Mary Doyle*
George Shiels: *Bedmates; Insurance Money*
Nikolai Evreinov: *A Merry Death*
Emile Maxaud: *The Perfect Day*

1922
MM Brennan: *The Young Man from

Rathmines; The Leprecaun in the Tenement
Padraic Colum and EWFreund: *The
Grasshopper*
Dorothy MacArdle: *Ann Kavanagh*
TC Murray: *Aftermath*
RJ Ray: *The Moral Law*
Lennox Robinson: *The Round Table;
Crabbed Youth and Age*
George Shiels: *Paul Twyning*
George Bernard Shaw: *The Man of Destiny*

1923
George Fitzmaurice: *'Twixt the Giltenans
and the Carmodys*
Augusta Gregory: *The Old Woman
Remembers*
JB McCarthy: *The Long Road to
Garranbraher*
Brinsley Macnamara: *The Glorious
Uncertainty*
Sean O'Casey: *The Shadow of a Gunman;
Cathleen Listens In*
Fand O'Grady: *Apartments*
George Shiels: *First Aid*
Oliver Goldsmith: *She Stoops to Conquer*
Henrik Ibsen: *A Doll's House*

1924
Augusta Gregory: *The Story Brought by
Brigit*
TC Murray: *Autumn Fire*
Sean O'Casey: *Juno and the Paycock;
Nannie's Night Out*
Lennox Robinson: *Never the Time and
the Place*
Kenneth Sarr: *The Passing; Old Mag*
George Shiels: *The Retrievers*
G Martinez Sierra: *The Two Shepherds; The
Kingdom of God*

1925
Dorothy MacArdle: *The Old Man*
FJH O'Donnell: *Anti-Christ*
Lennox Robinson: *Portrait in Two Sittings;
The White Blackbird*
George Shiels: *Professor Tim*
Anton Chekhov: *The Proposal*
George Bernard Shaw: *Fanny's First Play*

1926
Elizabeth Harte: *Mr Murphy's Island*
Brinsley Macnamara: *Look at the Heffernans!*
Sean O'Casey: *The Plough and the Stars*
Lennox Robinson: *The Big House*
WB Yeats: *Sophocles' King Oedipus*
Augusta Gregory: *The Would-Be Gentleman*
(from Molière)

Eugene O'Neill: *In the Zone*
Jules Romains: *Dr Knock*
Oscar Wilde: *The Importance of Being Earnest*

1927
Augusta Gregory: *Sancho's Master*; *Dave*
John Guinan: *Black Oliver*
MC Madden: *Parted*
TC Murray: *The Pipe in the Fields*
Arthur Power: *The Drapier Letters*
George Shiels: *Cartney and Kevney*
WB Yeats: *Sophocles' Oedipus at Colonnus*
Susan Glaspel: *Trifles*
Eugene O'Neill: *The Emperor Jones*
George Bernard Shaw: *Caesar and Cleopatra*

1928
Gerald Brosnan: *Before Midnight*
Brinsley Macnamara: *The Master*
TC Murray: *The Blind Wolf*
Cathleen O'Brennan: *Full Measure*
Lennox Robinson: *The Far-Off Hills*
Henrik Ibsen: *John Gabriel Borkman*
S and J Alvarez Quintero: *The Women Have their Way*
William Shakespeare: *King Lear*

1929
Gerald Brosnan: *Dark Isle*
Edward Dunsany: *The Gods of the Mountain*
Margaret O'Leary: *The Woman*
Lennox Robinson: *Ever the Twain*
George Shiels: *Mountain Dew*
WB Yeats: *Fighting the Waves*

1930
Paul Vincent Carroll: *The Watched Pot*
Bryan Cooper: *Let the Credit Go*
Teresa Deevy: *The Reapers*
Rutherford Mayne: *Peter*
George Shiels: *The New Gossoon*
WB Yeats: *The Words upon the Window Pane*

1931
Teresa Deevy: *A Disciple*
John Guinan: *The Rune of Healing*
Denis Johnston: *The Moon in the Yellow River*
A Leprovost: *Peter the Liar*
JA O'Brennan: *Scrap*
HP Quinn: *Money*
WB Yeats: *The Cat and the Moon*; *The Dreaming of the Bones*
George Bernard Shaw: *The Admirable Bashville*

1932
MM Brennan: *The Big Sweep*

Paul Vincent Carroll: *Things That Are Caesar's*
Teresa Deevy: *Temporal Powers*
AP Fanning: *Vigil*
TC Murray: *Michaelmas Eve*
Peadar O'Donnell: *Wrack*
Lennox Robinson: *All's Over Then*
GH Stafford: *The Mating of Shan M'Ghie*
Norman Webb: *Sheridan's Mills*
Henrik Ibsen: *The Wild Duck*

1933
Arthur Duff: *The Drinking Horn*
Brinsley Macnamara: *Margaret Gillan*
JK Montgomery: *The Jezebel*
FX O'Leary: *1920*
Lennox Robinson: *Drama at Inish*
George Shiels: *Grogan and the Ferret*
Frances Stuart: *Men Crowd Me Round*
George Bernard Shaw: *You Never Can Tell*

1934
WF Fearon: *Parnell of Avondale*
Rutherford Mayne: *Bridgehead*
Arthur Power: *The Marriage Packet*
Lennox Robinson: *Church Street*
WB Yeats: *The Resurrection*; *The King of the Great Clock Tower*
JPB Molière : *The School for Wives*
GK Munroe: *At Mrs Beam's*
Eugene O'Neill: *Days without End*
Luigi Pirandello: *Six Characters in Search of an Author*
Arthur Schnitzler: *Gallant Cassian*
William Shakespeare: *Macbeth*
George Bernard Shaw: *On the Rocks*

1935
Teresa Deevy: *The King of Spain's Daughter*
FR Higgins: *A Deuce o' Jacks*
Maura Molloy: *Summer's Day*
André Obey: *Noah*
Sean O'Casey: *The Silver Tassie*
José Maria Penham: *A Saint in a Hurry*
George Bernard Shaw: *A Village Wooing*; *Candida*

1936
Teresa Deevy: *Katie Roche*; *The Wild Goose*
Denis Johnston: *Blind Man's Buff* (from Toller)
Brinsley Macnamara: *The Grand House in the City*
Maeve O'Callaghan: *Wind from the West*
Cormac O'Daly: *The Silver Jubilee*
George Shiels: *The Passing Day*; *The Jailbird*
St John Ervine: *Boyd's Shop*
James Elroy Flecker: *Hassan*
William Shakespeare: *Coriolanus*

1937
Paul Vincent Carroll: *Shadow and Substance*; *Coggerers*
Louis D'Alton: *The Man in the Cloak*
Maura Molloy: *Who Will Remember…?*
'NOB': *The Phoenix*
Maeve O'Callaghan: *The Patriot*
Sean O'Casey: *The End of the Beginning*
Frank O'Connor and Hugh Hunt: *In the Train*; *The Invincibles*
Sean O Faoláin: *She Had to Do Something*
Lennox Robinson: *Killycreggs in Twilight*
George Shiels: *Quin's Secret*
Mervyn Wall: *Alarm among the Clerks*

1938
Charles Foley: *The Great Adventure*
Andrew Ganly: *The Dear Queen*
TC Murray: *A Spot in the Sun*
Frank O'Connor: *Time's Pocket*
Frank O'Connor and Hugh Hunt: *Moses' Rock*
Lennox Robinson: *Bird's Nest*
Mary Rynne: *Pilgrims*
George Shiels: *Neal Macquade*
Séamus Wilmot: *Baintighearna an Ghorta*
Jack B Yeats: *Harlequin's Positions*
WB Yeats: *Purgatory*
Douglas Hyde: *Casadh an t-Sugáin*

1939
EF Carey: *Caesar's Image*
Frank Carney: *They Went by the Bus*
Paul Vincent Carroll: *Kindred*
Daniel Corkery: *Fonham the Sculptor*
Louis D'Alton: *Tomorrow Never Comes*
JK Montgomery: *The Heritage*
TC Murray: *Illumination*
Séamus O hAodha: *Donnchadh Ruadh*
George Shiels: *Give him a House*

1940
Louis D'Alton: *The Spanish Soldier*
Frank Carney: *Peeping Tom*
Elizabeth Connor: *Mount Prospect*
St John Ervine: *William John Mawhinney*
Olga Feilden: *Three to Go*
WD Hempenstall: *Today and Yesterday*
Nora MacAdam: *The Birth of a Giant*
George Shiels: *The Rugged Path*
Francis Stuart: *Strange Guest*

1941
Austin Clarke: *Black Fast*
Elizabeth Connor: *Swans and Geese*
Louis D'Alton: *The Money Doesn't Matter*; *Lovers' Meeting*
St John Ervine: *Friends and Relations*

PJ Fitzgibbon: *The Fire Burns Late*
Brinsley Macnamara: *The Three Thimbles*
Bernard McGinn: *Remembered for Ever*
Roger McHugh: *Trial at Green Street Court House*
Lennox Robinson: *Forget-me-not*
George Shiels: *The Summit*
Mervyn Wall: *The Lady in the Twilight*

1942
Earnán de Blaghd: *Cách*
Elizabeth Connor: *An Apple a Day*
Andrew Ganly: *The Cursing Fields*
BG McCarthy: *The Whip Hand*
Traolach O Raithbheartaigh: *Gloine an Impire*
Padraic Pearse: *The Singer*
George Shiels: *The Fort Field*
Jack B Yeats: *La La Noo*
Alexander Ostrovsky: *An Stoirm* (tr. Aodh MacDubháin)

1943
Piaras Béaslaoi: *An Bhean Cródha*
'Myles na gCopaleen' (Flann O'Brien): *Faustus Kelly*
Seamus de Faoite: *An Traona sa Mhoinfhear* (tr. Fachtna O hAnnracháin)
Gerard Healy: *Thy Dear Father*
MJ Molloy: *Old Road*
Micheál O hAodha: *Ordóg an Bháis*
Roibeáed O Faracháin: *Assembly at Druim Ceat; Lost Light*
Tomas O Suilleabháin: *An Coimisinéar*
Anthony Wharton: *The O'Cuddy*
JJ Bernard: *Ar an mBóthar Mór* (tr. Liam O Bríain)
Marian Hemar: *Poor Man's Miracle* (tr. FB Czarnomski)

1944
Paul Vincent Carroll: *The Wise Have Not Spoken*
Ralph Kennedy: *Railway House*
Peadar O hAnnracháin: *Stiana*
Seán O Conchobhair: *Borumha Laighean*
Margaret O'Leary: *The Coloured Balloon*
George Shiels: *The New Regime*
Eibhlín ní Shuilleabháin: *Laistiar de'n Eadan*
Joseph Tomelty: *The End House*
JBP Molière: *Sodar i nDiadh na nUasal* (tr. Earnán de Blaghd)

1945
Liam MacBrádaigh: *An t-Udar in nGleic*
Roger McHugh: *Rossa*
Brinsley Macnamara: *Marks and Mabel*
Micheál O hAodha: *Muireann agus an Prionnsa*

Gregory O Bríain: *An t-Ubhall Oir*
George Shiels: *Tenants at Will*
René Fauchois: *Nuair a bhíonn Fear Marbh* (tr. Liam O Bríain)

1946
Frank Carney: *The Righteous Are Bold*
Walter Macken: *Mungo's Mansions*
MJ Molloy: *The Visiting House*
Pantomime: *Fernando agus an Dragan*
Daniel Corkery: *An Bunnan Buidhe* (tr. P O Domhnaill)
Augusta Gregory: *Cara an Phobail* (tr. M O Droighneáin)
TC Murray: *Oidreacht* (tr. Máire ni Shiothcháin)
George Shiels: *The Old Broom*
WB Yeats: *Caitlín ní Ullacháin* (tr. Tomás Luibhéid)

1947
Sigerson Clifford: *The Great Pacificator*
Elizabeth Connor: *The Dark Road*
Louis D'Alton: *They Got What They Wanted*
Roibeárd O Braonáin: *Oiche Mhaith Agut, a Mhic Uí Dhomhnaill* (tr. Liam O Bríain)
Maurice Baring: *Caitriona Parr* (tr. Liam O Laoghaire)
Anton Chekhov: *Cursaí Cleamhais* (tr. Muiris O Cathain)
Micheál MacLíammóir: *Diarmuid agus Gráinne*

1948
John Coulter: *The Drums Are Out*
Teresa Deevy: *Light Falling*
MJ Molloy: *The King of Friday's Men*
TC Murray: *The Briery Gap*
Arthur Power: *The Barn Dance*
Lennox Robinson: *The Lucky Finger*
Terence Smith: *Cavaliero*
Pantomimes: *Réalt Dhiarmuda; Brian agus an Claidheamh Soluis*
JM Barrie: *Máire Rós* (tr. Siobhán Nic Chionnaith)
Erckermann-Chatrian: *Na Cloigíní* (tr. Maighread Nic Mhaicín)
André Ghéon: *Arís* (tr. Liam O Bríain)
MJ McHugh: *Moill na Mithidí* (tr. Gobnait ní Loinsigh)
Gerard de Nerval: *Nicolas Flamel* (tr. Seamus O Sullivan)

1949
Ralph Kennedy: *Ask for Me Tomorrow*
Bryan MacMahon: *The Bugle in the Blood*
Mary Davenport O'Neill: *War, the Monster*
Joseph Tomelty: *All Souls' Night*
Jack B Yeats: *In Sand*
Pantomime: *Niall agus Carmelita*

Jacinte Benevente: *Bean an Mhí-ghrá* (tr. Padraigín ni Néill)
Anton Chekhov: *An Béar*
Douglas Hyde: *An Pósadh*
Federico García Lorca: *Blood Wedding*
Micheál MacLíammóir: *Oiche Bhealtaine*

1950
Seamus Byrne: *Design for a Headstone*
JackP Cunningham: *Mountain Flood*
Donal Giltinan: *The Goldfish in the Sun*
Aindreas O Gallchobhair: *Clocha na Coigherice*
Pantomime: *Una agus Jimín*
Joseph Bédier: *Tristan agus Isialt* (tr. Louis Artus Don Piatt)
Federico Garcia Lorca: *The House of Barnarda Alba*

1951
Eamon Guallí: *Ais na nDéithe*
Maurice Meldon: *The House under Green Shadows*
William Boyle: *Na Ciste Tógála* (tr. Piaras MacLochlain)
André Ghéon: *Geamaireacht Droichid an Diabhail* (tr. Liam O Bríain)
Pierre Jalabert: *Na Cruiteacháin* (tr. Liam O Bríain)

After the fire which destroyed the original building on 17 July 1951 the company performed temporarily at the Rupert Guinness Hall where one new play was presented:

Louis D'Alton: *The Devil a Saint Would Be*

The company reopened at the Queen's Theatre on 24 August 1951 where the following plays received their first productions:

Seamus Byrne: *Innocent Bystander*
Anne Daly: *Window on the Square*
Pantomime: *Réamonn agus Niamh Og*

1952
Donal Giltinan: *The Gentle Maiden*
Walter Macken: *Home Is the Hero*
Pantomime: *Setanta agus an Chú*
Harold Brighouse: *An Crann Ubhall* (tr. Seamus O Tuama)
Augusta Gregory: *Eirí na Gealaí* (tr. Tomás MacAnna)
George Shiels: *Ag Baint Lae As* (tr. Seán Toibin)

1953
Louis D'Alton: *This Other Eden*
Mairéad ni Ghráda: *Lá Buí Bealtaine*

Tomás MacAnna: *A Fear a phós Balbhán*
(music: Gearóid Mac an Bhuaidh)
MJ Molloy: *The Wood of the Whispering; The Paddy Pedlar*
Séamus O hAodha: *An Luch Tuaithe*
Pantomime: *Bláithín agus an Mac Rí*
Francois Coppée: *An Duais-Bheidhlín* (tr. Tomás MacAnna)

1954
JM Doody: *Knocknavain*
Bryan Guinness: *A Riverside Charade*
John Malone: *John Courtney*
John McCann: *Twenty Years A-Wooing*
John O'Donovan: *The Half-Millionaire*
Pantomime: *Sonia agus an Bodach*
Joseph Tomelty: *Is the Priest at Home?*

1955
Risteárd de Paor: *Saoirse*
Mairéad ni Ghráda: *Ull Glas Oíchne Shamhna*
Walter Macken: *Twilight of a Warrior*
John McCann: *Blood is Thicker than Water*
Pauline Maguire: *The Last Move*
MJ Molloy: *The Will and the Way*
Pantomime: *Ulyssés agus Penelopé*
Mathew Bolton: *An Murlán Práis* (tr. Earnán de Blaghd)

1956
Denis Johnston: *Strange Occurrence on Ireland's Eye*
Hugh Leonard: *The Big Birthday*
Gearóid MacAn Bhuaithe: *Iomrall Aithne*
Tomás MacAnna: *Winter Wedding*
John McCann: *Early and Often*
Francis MacManus: *Judgement in James O'Neill*
Seán O Tuama: *Gunna Camh agus Sliabhra Oir*
Pantomime: *An Cruiscín Lán*
Brendan Behan: *The Quare Fella*

1957
Niall Carroll: *The Wanton Tide*
Donal Giltinan: *The Flying Wheel*
PS Laughlin: *Waiting Night*
Hugh Leonard: *A Leap in the Dark*
Labhrás MacBrádaigh: *Céad Feadha Síos*
John McCann: *Give Me a Bed of Roses*
John O'Donovan: *The Less We Are Together*
Pantomime: *Muireann agus an Prionnsa*

1958
Risteárd de Paor: *An Oighreacht*
Denis Johnston: *The Scythe and the Sunset*
MJ Molloy: *A Right Rose Tree*
Séamus O Ceallaigh: *An Briob*
John O'Donovan: *A Change of Mind*

James Plunkett: *The Risen People*
Niall Sheridan: *Seven Men and a Dog*
Pantomime: *Oisín i dTír na nOg*
Louis D'Alton: *Cafflin' Johnny*
Padraic MacPiarais: *Iosagáin*
'An Seabhac': *An Strainsear*
Marjorie Watson: *Ar Buille a hOcht* (tr. Tomás MacAnna)
WB Yeats: *Pota an Anraith* (tr. Breandan O hEithir)

1959
Tomás Coffey: *Stranger, Beware*
Ann Daly: *Leave it to the Doctor*
Mairéad ní Ghráda: *Sugán Sneachta*
Peter Hutchinson: *No Man Is an Island*
John McCann: *I Know Where I'm Going*
John Murphy: *The Country Boy*
Criostóir O Floinn: *In Dublin's Fair City*
Pantomime: *Gráinne na Long*
Eugene O'Neill: *Long Day's Journey into Night*
John D Stewart: *Danger, Men Working*

1960
Anthony Butler: *The Deputy's Daughter*
Tomás Coffey: *Anyone Can Rob a Bank*
Sean Dowling: *The Bird in the Net*
Mairéad ní Ghráda: *Mac Uí Rudaí*
Bryan MacMahon: *The Song of the Anvil*
John McCann: *It Can't Go On For Ever*
John O'Donovan: *The Shaws of Synge Street*
Pantomime: *An Sciath Draíochta*
St John Ervine: *The Lady of Belmont*
JBP Molière: *An Doctúir Bréige*
JM Synge: *Chun an Farraige Síos* (tr. Tomás O Muircheartaigh agus Séamus O Sé)

1961
Eamonn Cassidy: *Brave Banner*
Tom Coffey: *The Long Sorrow*
Richard Johnson: *The Evidence I Shall Give*
Bryan MacMahon: *The Honey Spike*
John McCann: *Put a Beggar on Horseback*
John McDonnell: *All the King's Horses*
Michael Murphy: *Men on the Wall*
Pantomime: *Diarmuid agus Balor*
Betty Barr and Gould Stevens: *An Fear Og Umhal Malda* (tr. Eoin O Súilleabháin)

1962
Kevin Casey: *The Living and the Lost*
Brian Friel: *The Enemy Within*
Donal Giltinan: *A Light in the Sky*
John B Keane: *Hut 42*
Liam Lynch: *Do Thrushes Sing in Birmingham?*
Séamus MacMánais: *Liudaí Og na Láirge Móire*

John McCann: *A Jew Called Sammy*
Pantomime: *An Claíomh Soluis*
Gerald Macnamara: *Thompson in Tír na nOg*
Eugene O'Neill: *Ah, Wilderness*

1963
Michael Mulvihill: *A Sunset Touch*
John O'Donovan: *Copperfaced Jack*
Pantomime: *Flann agus Clementín*
John B Keane: *The Man from Clare*
Reinhardt Rafflat: *The Successor* (tr. Steven Vas)

1964
Cyril Daly: *A Matter of Practice*
Eilís Dillon: *A Page of History*
MJ Molloy: *The Wooing of Duvesa*
Pantomime: *Aisling as Tír na nOg*
Stewart Love: *The Big Long Bender*

1965
Sean Dowling: *The Best of Motives*
Arnold Hill: *The Pilgrim's Mother*
Liam MacUistin: *Coiriú na Leapan*
Eoin Neeson and Colm McNeill: *The Face of Treason*
Pantomime: *Emer agus an Laoch*
Bertolt Brecht: *The Life of Galileo*

1966
Tom Coffey: *The Call*
Kenneth Deale: *The Conspiracy*
Sean O'Casey: *The Hall of Healing*
John Power: *The Irishwoman of the Year*
Federico García Lorca: *Yerma* (tr. James Graham-Lujan and Richard O'Connell)

The company's final performance at the Queen's Theatre took place on 9 July 1966. The building housing the new Abbey and Peacock Theatres was opened on 18 July, with initially only the Abbey stage in operation.

Michael Judge: *Death Is for Heroes*
Walter Macken: *Recall the Years*
P J O'Connor: *Tarry Flynn* (from Patrick Kavanagh)
Louis MacNeice: *One for the Grave*
Pantomime: *Fernando agus an Ríonn Og*

From 26 July 1967 the Peacock Theatre was in a full-time operation. Henceforth both the Abbey and Peacock stages have been in continuous production throughout the year. First performances of original plays remain in bold type, while the Company's first performances of plays which had previously been produced are in lighter type, irrespective of whether the play in question appeared on the Abbey or Peacock stage.

1967

James McKenna: *At Bantry*
Frank McMahon: *Borstal Boy* (from Brendan Behan)
John O'Donovan: *Dearly Beloved Roger*
Padraig O Giollagáin: *An Choinneal*
Séamus O'Neill: *Faill ar an Bhfeart*
Samuel Beckett: *Play*; *Film*
Dion Boucicault: *The Shaughran*; *An Cailín Bán* (tr. Liam O Bríain)
George Fitzmaurice: *The Magic Glasses*
Brian Friel: *The Loves of Cass Maguire*
Seán O Bríain: *An Béal Bocht* (from Flann O'Brien)
Sean O'Casey: *Red Roses for Me*

1968

Mairéad ní Ghráda: *Breithiúntas*
Michael Judge: *An Baile seo Gainne* (from 'An Seabhac')
Fergus Linehan and Tomás MacAnna: *The Sound of the Gong*
Mary Manning: *The Saint and Mary Kate* (from Flann O'Brien)
Tom Murphy: *Famine*
Criostóir O Floinn: *Is é Dúirt Polónius*
PJ O'Connor: *The Tailor and Ansty* (from Eric Cross)
MD Power: *The General's Watch*
Jack White: *The Last Eleven*
Samuel Beckett: *Come and Go*
Brendan Behan: *An Giall*
Anton Chekhov: *The Cherry Orchard*
Jean Genet: *The Maids*
Frank D Gilroy: *The Subject Was Roses*
Donagh MacDonagh: *Happy as Larry*
Eugene O'Neill: *Before Breakfast*

1969

Conor Farrington: *Aaron thy Brother*
George Fitzmaurice: *The Dandy Dolls*
Thomas Kilroy: *The O'Neill*
Liam Lynch: *Soldier*
Tomas MacAnna: *Séadna* (from Peadar O Laoghaire)
Eugene McCabe: *Swift*
Tom Murphy: *A Crucial Week in the Life of a Grocer's Assistant*
Micheál O hAodha: *The Weaver's Grave* (from Seumas O'Kelly)
Joe O'Donnell: *Let the Ravens Feed*
Diarmuid O Suilleabháin: *An Deisceart Domhain*

Samuel Beckett: *Waiting for Godot*
Austin Clarke: *The Second Kiss*
Frank McMahon: *The Fiery Gates*
WB Yeats: *The Countess Cathleen*

1970

Wesley Burrowes: *The Becauseway*
Sydney Cheatle: *The Director*; *Retreat*
Tomás MacAnna, John D Stewart and Eugene Watters: *A State of Chassis*
Audrey Welsh: *At Swim-Two-Birds* (from Flann O'Brien)
Samuel Beckett: *Krapp's Last Tape*
Brendan Behan: *The Hostage*
Anton Chekhov: *The Seagull*
Gunter Grass: *The Plebeians Rehearse the Uprising* (tr. Ralph Manheim)
Peter Luke: *Hadrian VII*
Eugene McCabe: *King of the Castle*
Micheál MacLíammóir: *Tá Crut Nua ar na Sléibhte* (tr. Liam O Bríain)
Harold Pinter: *The Lover*; *The Dumb Waiter*

1971

Wesley Burrowes: *A Loud Bang on June 1st*
Padraic Fallon: *Sweet Love till Morn*
Constantine Fitzgibbon: *The Devil at Work*
GP Gallivan: *The Dáil Debate*
Tomás MacAnna and Seán O Bríain: *Dragán '71*
Liam MacUistin: *Pocléim*
Tom Murphy: *The Morning after Optimism*
Tom Tessier: *The Rose in the Fisted Glove*
Jack White: *Today the Bullfinch*
Fernando Arrabal: *Fando and Lis*
Marjorie Barkentin: *Ulysses in Nighttown* (from James Joyce)
JP Donleavy: *Fairy Tales of New York*
Lin Ford: *The Serpent Prince*; *The Blue Demon*
Harold Pinter: *The Homecoming*
JM Synge: *The Tinker's Wedding*

1972

Brendan Behan: *Richard's Cork Leg*
Frank Harvey: *They Feed Christians to Lions Here, Don't They?*
Tom MacIntyre: *Eye Winker Tom Tinker*
Heno Magee: *Hatchet*
Tom Murphy: *The White House*
Pádraig O Giollagáin: *Fleadh*
Edward Rowe: *Splinters from a Glass*
Richard Stockton and Richard Herd: *Prisoner of the Crown*
Fernando Arrabal: *Picnic on the Battlefield*
Dion Boucicault: *Arrah-na-Pogue*
Brian Friel: *Philadelphia, Here I Come!*
Tomás MacAnna and Eamon Kelly: *Scéal Scéalaí*

Eugene McCabe: *Pull Down a Horseman*
Sean O'Casey: *Bedtime Story*
Eugene O'Neill: *The Iceman Cometh*
Harold Pinter: *Old Times*
George Bernard Shaw: *Saint Joan*
Paul Shephard: *An Evening In*
August Strindberg: *Easter*

1973

Helen Cahill: *The Doll in the Gap*
Brian Friel: *The Freedom of the City*
Wilson John Haire: *The Bloom of the Diamond Stone*
Tomás MacAnna: *Dear Edward*
Tomás MacAnna and Eamon Kelly: *Scéal Scéalaí Eile*
Heno Magee: *Red Biddy*
Conor Cruise O'Brien: *King Herod Explains*
Criostóir O Floinn: *Mise Raufteirí an File*
Pádraig O Giollagáin: *Johnny Orfeo*
Sean Walsh: *The Night of the Rouser*
Samuel Beckett: *Happy Days*
Maureen Duffy: *Rites*
Patrick Duggan: *The Golden Horseshoe*
Jean Genet: *Death Watch*
Michel de Ghelderode: *Escurial*
James Joyce: *Exiles*
Thomas Kilroy: *The Death and Resurrection of Mr Roche*
Donagh MacDonagh: *God's Gentry*
TC Murray: *Laom Luinse Fomhair* (tr. Micheál O Siichfhradha)
Richard Brinsley Sheridan: *The School for Scandal*
WB Yeats: *The Herne's Egg*

1974

James Ballantine: *Sarah*
Wesley Burrowes: *The Truth in the News*
Hugh Carr: *The Life and Times of Benvenuto Cellini*
Peadar MacGiolla Cearr: *The Food of Love*
Henry Comerford: *One Is One and All Alone*
John McKendrick: *Struensee*
Tom Murphy: *The Vicar of Wakefield* (from Goldsmith)
Edna O'Brien: *The Gathering*
Jim Sheridan: *The Happy-Go-Likeable Man* (from Molière)
Sean Walsh: *Earwig*
John Antrobus: *The Missing Links*
Fernando Arrabal: *The Architect and the Emperor of Assyria*
Bertolt Brecht: *The Resistible Rise of Arturo Uí*
Anton Chekhov: *Three Sisters*
Lyn Ford: *Witches's Brew*
Don Haworth: *The Illumination of Mr Shannon*

Eduardo Manet: *Them*
Luigi Pirandello: *The Man with a Flower in his Mouth*
David Storey: *Home*
August Strindberg: *Motherlove*
Tennessee Williams: *The Glass Menagerie*

1975
Brian Friel: *Volunteers*
Ernest Gebler: *Cry for Help*
Kevin Grattan: *Ryyming Couplets*
Desmond Hogan: *A Short Walk to the Sea*
Eamon Kelly: *In My Father's Time*
**Fergus Linehan and Jim Doherty: *Innish*
(from Lennox Robinson)**
Tom Murphy: *The Sanctuary Lamp*
Sean O'Casey: *Figuro in the Night*
Ulick O'Connor: *Deirdre*
Fernando Arrabal: *The Two Executioners*
Robert Pinguet: *The Old Tune; Architruc*
Luigi Pirandello: *Dreaming (Or Am I?)*
Sean O'Casey: *Purple Dust*
William Shakespeare: *Twelfth Night*

1976
Maeve Binchy: *End of Term*
May Cluskey: *Mothers*
George Fitzmaurice: *The Enchanted Land*
Desmond Hogan: *Sanctified Distances*
Eamon Kelly: *Bless Me, Father…*
Thomas Kilroy: *Tea and Sex and Shakespeare*
Pat Layde: *The Hard Life* (from Flann O'Brien)
Hugh Leonard: *Time Was*
John Lynch: *All You Need Is Love*
Tomás MacAnna and others: *Mise le Meas*
Tom MacIntyre: *Jack Be Nimble*
Kevin O'Connor: *Friends*
Sean Walsh: *The Whipping*
Campbell Black: *They Used to Star in Movies*
Brian Friel: *Lovers*
Eugene O'Neill: *Desire under the Elms*
Harold Pinter: *The Birthday Party*
William Shakespeare: *Much Ado about Nothing*
Richard Brinsley Sheridan: *The Rivals*
John Whiting: *The Devils*
Thornton Wilder: *Our Town*

1977
Brian Friel: *Living Quarters*
Thomas Kilroy: *Talbot's Box*
Tom MacIntyre: *Find the Lady*
**Bill Morrison: *The Emperor of Ice Cream*
(from Brian Moore)**

Eoghan O Tuairisc: *Aisling mhic Artain; Oisín*
Stewart Parker: *Catchpenny Twist; The Actress and the Bishop*
**Sean Walsh: *Manus and the Mighty Dragon*
(from Augusta Gregory)**
Jules Feiffer: *Little Murders*
Denis Johnston: *The Old Lady Says 'No!'*
Edna O'Brien: *A Pagan Place*
Bill Morrison: *Conn and the Conquerors of Space*
Sean O'Casey: *Cock-a-Doodle Dandy*
John O'Keefe: *Wild Oats*
William Shakespeare: *Measure for Measure*
George Bernard Shaw: *Mrs Warren's Profession*
Tom Stoppard: *Travesties*

1978
Pat Ingoldsby: *Hisself; When Am I Getting me Clothes?; Rhymin' Simon*
Eamon Kelly: *A Rub of the Relic*
Eamon Morrissey: *Patrick Gulliver*
Pádraig O Giollagáin; *An Gabha go Raibh*
Pascal Petit: *Catapletits*
Samuel Beckett: *Act without Words; That Time*
Anton Chekhov: *Uncle Vanya; Ivanov*
Carlo Goldoni: *The Servant of Two Masters*
Hugh Leonard: *Stephen D* (from James Joyce)
Arthur Miller: *The Crucible*
JBP Molière: *The Misanthrope* (tr. Harrison)
Sean O'Casey: *The Star Turns Red*
George Bernard Shaw: *You Never Can Tell*

1979
Leland Bardwell: *Open-Ended Prescription*
Maeve Binchy: *The Half-Promised Land*
Tony Browne: *The Contrivance*
Hugh Carr: *Goodbye, Sam Maguire*
Bernard Farrell: *I Do Not Like Thee, Dr Fell*
Brian Friel: *Aristocrats*
Jennifer Johnston: *The Nightingale and Not the Lark*
Eamon Kelly: *The Story Goes*
Tomás MacAnna: *Táinbocú*
MJ Molloy: *Petticoat Loose*
Eamon Morrissey: *The Brother*
Tom Murphy: *Epitaph under Ether*
Hugh Leonard: *A Life*
MacDara O Fátharta: *Deoraíocht* (from Padraig O Conaire)
Graham Reid: *The Death of Humpty Dumpty*
Edward Bond: *The Sea*
James Douglas: *A Tale after School*
Georges Feydeau: *A Flea in her Ear*
Eugene McCabe: *Gale Day*
Wolf Mankowitz: *The Bespoke Overcoat*

John Molloy: *From the Vikings to Bang Bang*
Stephen Poliakoff: *City Sugar*
William Shakespeare: *A Midsummer Night's Dream*
Tennessee Williams: *Portrait of a Madonna*

1980
Neil Donnelly: *Upstarts*
Bernard Farrell: *Canaries*
Lin Ford: *Snake-eye and the Diamond*
Sean McCarthy: *Dan Phaidí Aindi* (from John B Keane)
Eamon Kelly: *English That for Me*
Tomás MacAnna: *Glittering Spears*
Eamon Morrissey: *Joycemen*
Tom Murphy: *The Blue Macushla*
MacDara O Fátharta: *Lig Sin I gCathú* (from Breandán O hEithir)
Stewart Parker: *Nightshade*
Graham Reid: *The Closed Door*
George Kaufman and Moss Hart: *The Man Who Came to Dinner*
William Shakespeare: *The Winter's Tale*
John Steinbeck: *Of Mice and Men*

1981
Martin Boylan: *Thompsons*
Eilís Dillon: *The Cats' Opera*
Neil Donnelly: *The Silver Dollar Boys*
Bernard Farrell: *All in Favour Said No!*
Eamon Kelly: *A Rogue of Low Degree*
Sean McCarthy: *Childish Things*
Colm O Dálaigh: *Fiche Bliain ag Fás* (from Muiris O Suilleabháin)
Antoine O Flatharta: *Gaeilgeoirí*
William Trevor: *Scenes from an Album*
Samuel Beckett: *Footfalls; Not I; Play*
Brian Friel: *Faith Healer*
Barrie Keefe: *Gotcha!*
James McClure: *Lone Star*
Sam Shepard: *Buried Child*
Tom Stoppard: *Night and Day*

1982
Bernard Farrell: *Petty Sessions* (from Boucicault)
Desmond Forristal: *Kolbe*
Pat Ingoldsby: *Yeukface the Yeuk and the Spotty Grousler*
Fergus Linehan: *Stone Mad* (from Seamus Murphy)
Fergus and Rosaleen Linehan: *Mary Makebelieve* (from James Stephens)
Sean McCarthy: *A Doll's House* (from Ibsen)
Frank McGuinness: *The Factory Girls*
Tom Murphy: *She Stoops to Conquer* (from Goldsmith)

Graham Reid: *The Hidden Curriculum*
Brian Friel: *Philadelphia, Here I Come!*
Tom Gallacher: *Mr Joyce Is Leaving Paris*
James McClure: *Pvt. Wars*; *Laundry and Bourbon*
Murray Schisgal: *The Pushcart Peddlers*

1983
Jim Doherty: *The Lugnaquilla Gorilla*
Neil Donnelly: *Flying Home*
James Douglas: *Pisces the Cod*
Bernard Farrell: *Don Juan* (from Molière)
Mary Gallagher: *Chocolate Cake*
Eamon Kelly: *Your Humble Servant*
Fergus Linehan: *Hotel Casanova* (from Georges Feydeau)
Tom MacIntyre: *The Great Hunger* (from Patrick Kavanagh)
Aodhan Madden: *The Midnight Door*
Tom Murphy: *The Gigli Concert*
Antoine O Flatharta: *Imeachtaí na Saoirse*
Robert Packer: *The Unexpected Death of Jimmy Blizzard*
Tom Kempinski: *Duet for One*
Hugh Leonard: *Da*
Lanford Wilson: *Talley's Folly*
William Shakespeare: *Hamlet*
George Bernard Shaw: *Overruled*

1984
Richard J Byrne: *Auld Dacency*
Neil Donnelly: *Chalk Farm Blues*
Tomás MacAnna and Eamonn O Muirgheasa: *Gach Neach Beo*
Tom MacIntyre: *The Bearded Lady*
Eamonn Morrissey: *Mr Gulliver's Bags*
Siobhán Nic Chionnaith: *Cúirt and Mhean Oiche* (from Brian Merriman)
John Olohan: *Storytime*
Samuel Beckett: *Rockaby*
Beth Henley: *Crimes of the Heart*
Martin Lynch: *The Interrogation of Ambrose Fogarty*
William Shakespeare: *The Merchant of Venice*

1985
Bernard Farrell: *All the Way Back*
Eoghan Harris: *Souper Sullivan*
Tomás MacAnna and Eamonn O Muirgheasa: *Candide '85* (from Voltaire)
Tom MacIntyre: *Rise Up, Lovely Sweeney*
Frank McGuinness: *Observe the Sons of Ulster Marching towards the Somme*; *Bag Lady*
Ulick O Connor: *Executions*
John Olohan: *Storytime 2*

MacDara O Fátharta: *Castar na Daoine ar a Chéile*
Graham Reid: *Callers*
Lynn Roth: *Freud*
John B Keane: *Sive*
David Mamet: *Glengarry Glen Ross*
Sean O'Casey: *The Drums of Father Ned*

1986
Douglas Kennedy: *Send Lawyers, Guns and Money*
Brendan Kennelly: *Antigone* (from Sophocles)
Micheál MacCarthaigh: *Saol I mBás Phaidí Jeo*
Aodhan Madden: *Sensations*
Tom Murphy: *A Thief of a Christmas*
Ulick O'Connor: *Deirdre*
Antoine O Flatharta: *Ag Eaglain in Eireann*
George Farquhar: *The Beaux' Stratagem*
Hugh Leonard: *The Patrick Pearse Motel*
Nicolo Machiavelli: *Mandragola*
Tom Murphy: *A Whistle in the Dark*
Sam Shepard: *A Fool for Love*

1987
Bernard Farrell: *Say Cheese!*
Michael Harding: *Strawboys*
Jennifer Johnston: *The Invisible Man*
Frank McGuinness: *Yerma* (from Lorca)
Tom MacIntyre: *Dance for your Daddy*
Aodhan Madden: *Remember Mauretania*
Peter Sheridan: *Mother of All the Behans* (from Kathleen Behan)
Carolyn Swift: *Lady G*
Jean Anouilh: *Ring Round the Moon* (tr. Christopher Fry)
Stephen Berkoff: *The Fall of the House of Usher* (from Poe)
Donald Freed: *The Last Hero*
Vladimir Gubaryev: *Sarcophagus*
Peter Sheridan: *Dialann Ocrais*
Tom Stoppard: *Rozencrantz and Guildenstern Are Dead*
Dylan Thomas: *A Child's Christmas in Wales*

1988
Jean Binnie: *Colours*
Edward Callan: *I Am of Ireland*
Anthony Cronin and Ronnie Walsh: *Ulysses* (from James Joyce)
Tom MacIntyre: *Snow White*
Frank McGuinness: *Times in It*
Aiden C Mathews: *Exit Entrance*
Ulick O'Connor: *A Trinity of Two*
John B Keane: *Big Maggie*
William Philips: *St Stephen's Green*

1989
Sebastian Barry: *Boss Grady's Boys*
Neil Donnelly: *Goodbye, Carraroe*; *The Reel McCoy*
Robert Doyle: *A Friend of the Corpse*
Michael Harding: *Una Pooka*
Jennifer Johnston: *Triptych*
Sean Lawlor: *The Watchman*
Karl McDermott: *Memoirs of a Midget*
Tom Murphy: *Too Late for Logic*
Ulick O'Connor: *Joyicity*
Antoine O Flatharta: *Blood Guilty*
Brian Friel: *The Gentle Island*
Max Frisch: *Na Dóiteoirí*
Maxim Gorky: *The Lower Depths*
George S Kaufman and Moss Hart: *You Can't Take it with You*
Thomas Kilroy: *Ghosts* (from Henrik Ibsen)
Donal O'Kelly: *Bat the Father Rabbit the Son*
Eugene O'Neill: *Hughie*
George Bernard Shaw: *The Devil's Disciple*
Peter Sheridan and Jean Doyle: *Shades of the Jellywoman*
Thornton Wilder: *The Happy Journey from Trenton to Camden*

1990
Sebastian Barry: *Prayers of Sherkin*
Dermot Bolger: *Blinded by the Light*
Brian Friel: *Dancing at Lughnasa*
Michael Harding: *Misogynist*
Fergus Linehan: *Frauds*
Tom MacIntyre: *Kitty O'Shea*
Donal O'Kelly: *Mamie Sighs*
Alan Titley: *Tagann Godot*
Samuel Beckett: *Catastrophe*; *What Where*; *Nacht und Traume*

1991
Dermot Bolger: *One Last White Horse*
Marina Carr: *Ullaloo*
Alan Cullen: *Danny, the Witch and the Boggin*
Deirdre Hines: *Howling Moons, Silent Sons*
Tomás MacAnna and Eamon Kelly: *Má tá Bréag ann*
John McGahern: *The Power of Darkness* (from Leo Tolstoy)
Tom Murphy: *The Patriot Game*
Niall Williams: *The Murphy Initiative*
Dermot Bolger: *The Lament for Arthur Cleary*
Dion Boucicault: *The Corsican Brothers*
Henrik Ibsen: *Hedda Gabler* (tr. Una Ellis-Fermor)

1992
Sebastian Barry: *White Woman Street*
Hugh Leonard: *Moving*

Sean MacMathúna: *The Winter Thief/Gadaí Géar na Geamh-Oíche*
Rona Munro: *Bold Girls*
Antoine O Flatharta: *Silverlands*
Joseph Brodsky: *Democracy*
Tom Murphy: *Conversations on a Homecoming*
Janet Noble: *Away Alone*

1993

Bernard Farrell: *The Last Apache Reunion*
Brian Friel: *Wonderful Tennessee*
Michael Harding: *Hubert Murray's Widow*
Brendan Kennelly: *The Trojan Women* (from Euripides)
Jimmy Murphy: *Brothers of the Brush*
Billy Roche: *The Cavalcaders*
Gerry Stembridge: *Ceaussu's Ear*
Frank McGuinness: *Someone Who'll Watch Over Me*
Billy Roche: *The Wexford Trilogy*
William Shakespeare: *The Comedy of Errors*

1994

John Banville: *The Broken Jug* (from Heinrich von Kleist)
Marina Carr: *The Mai*
Michael Harding: *Ceacht Houdini*
Kevin Lavin: *Rumplestiltskin*
Hugh Leonard: *Chamber Music*
Eilis ní Dhuibhne: *Dún na mBan Trí Thine*
Frank McGuinness: *The Bird Sanctuary*
Tom MacIntyre: *Sheep's Milk on the Boil*
Donal O'Kelly: *Asylum! Asylum!*

1995

Sebastian Barry: *The Only True History of Lizzie Finn*
Dermot Bolger: *April Bright*
Neil Donnelly: *The Duty Master*
Clare Dowling: *Small City*
Katy Hayes: *Playgirl*
Kevin Lavin: *The Man Who Became a Legend*
Brian Lynch: *The Third Law of Motion*
Tom MacIntyre: *Good Evening, Mr Collins*
Pat McCabe: *The Adventures of Shay Mouse*
Antoine O Flatharta: *An Suas Dearc*
Colin Teevan: *Vinegar and Brown Paper*
Michael West: *Monkey*
Niall Williams: *A Little Like Paradise*
Tony Kushner: *Angels in America*

1996

Marina Carr: *Portia Coughlan*
Philip Davison: *The Invisible Mending Company*
Thomas Kilroy: *Six Characters in Search*

of an Author (from Pirandello)
John McArdle: *Something's in the Way*
Tom Murphy: *She Stoops to Folly* (from Goldsmith)
Antoine O Flatharta: *Strawberries in December*
Michael West: *The Marriage of Figaro* (from Beaumarchais)
Oscar Wilde: *A Woman of No Importance*

1997

Brian Fitzgibbon: *The Papar*
Brian Friel: *Give Me Your Answer, Do!*
Thomas Kilroy: *The Secret Fall of Constance Wilde*
Gary Mitchell: *In a Little World of our Own*
Alex Johnston: *Melonfarmer*
Noel MacAodh: *Respond*
Tom MacIntyre: *The Chirpaun*
Conall Morrison: *Tarry Flynn* (from Patrick Kavanagh)
Jimmy Murphy: *A Picture of Paradise*
Lorraine O'Brien: *A Different Rhyme*

1998

Marina Carr: *By the Bog of Cats*
Bernard Farrell: *Kevin's Bed*
Michael Harding: *Amazing Grace*
Dermot Healy, Pat McCabe and Eilis ní Dhuibhne: *Swans, Boots and Boxes*
Declan Hughes: *Twenty Grand*
Alex Johnston: *At Swim-Two-Birds* (from Flann O'Brien)
Chris Lee: *The Electrocution of Children*
Tom MacIntyre: *Caoineadh Airt Uí Laoghaire* (from Eibhlín ní Chonnaill)
Gary Mitchell: *As the Beast Sleeps*
Gina Moxley and David Bolger: *Toupées and Snare Drums*
Tom Murphy: *The Wake*

1999

Dermot Bolger: *The Passion of Jerome*
Darragh Carville: *Observatory*
Chris Lee: *The Map Maker's Sorrow*
Hugh Leonard: *Love in the Title*
Kathy McArdle and Andrea Ainsworth: *Sisters and Brothers*
Frank McGuinness: *Dolly West's Kitchen*
Tom MacIntyre: *Cúirt an Mhéan Oíche* (from Brian Merriman)
Donal O'Kelly: *Judas of the Gallarus*
William Shakespeare: *The Tempest*

2000

Jocelyn Clarke: *Alice's Adventures in*

Wonderland; Through the Looking Glass (from Lewis Carroll)
Declan Hughes: *Tartuffe* (from Molière)
Liz Kuti: *Tree Houses*
Frank McGuinness: *Barbaric Comedies* (from Ramón Maria del Valle-Inclán)
Kenneth McLeish and Frederick Raphael: *Medea* (from Euripides)
Tom Murphy: *The House*
Patrick Marber: *Closer*

2001

Ken Bourke: *The Hunt for Red Willie*
Nicholas Kelly: *A Quiet Life*
Jim Nolan: *Blackwater Angel*
Eugene O'Brien: *Eden*
Mark O'Rowe: *Made in China*
Billy Roche: *On Such As We*
Don Taylor: *Iphigenia at Aulis* (from Euripides)
Bertolt Brecht: *Mann ist Mann*
Tom Murphy: *Bailegangaire*
Shelagh Stephenson: *The Memory of Water*

2002

Sebastian Barry: *Hinterland*
Marina Carr: *Ariel*
Bernard Farrell: *Lovers at Versailles*
Ken Harmon: *Done Up Like a Kipper*
Aidan Mathews: *Communion*
Joe O'Byrne: *En Suite*
Gerard Stembridge: *That Was Then*
Michael West: *Lolita* (from Nabokov)
William Shakespeare: *Henry IV*
Michel Tremblay: *For the Pleasure of Seeing Her Again*

2003

Marina Carr and Jim Nolan: *Sons and Daughters*
Hilary Fannin: *Dolorum Bay*
Thomas Kilroy: *The Shape of Metal*
Sebastian Barry: *The House of Bernarda Alba* (from Lorca)
Frank McGuinness: *The Wild Duck* (from Ibsen)

acknowledgments

I wish to thank Ms Mairéad Delaney, Abbey Theatre archivist, for unremitting help and advice far beyond any imaginable call of duty; and also the theatre's press officer, Ms Lucy McKeever; the former general manager Mr Martin Fahy; and the former artistic director Mr Joe Dowling. The director of the National Library of Ireland, Mr Brendan O'Donoghue, and the staff of the reading room and manuscripts department, have been especially supportive; the director and staff of the National Gallery of Ireland and the director and staff of the Hugh Lane Municipal Gallery of Modern Art, Dublin, provided special courtesies; as did the director general of Radio Telefís Eireann. I gratefully acknowlege the assistance of Ms Mary Clark, Dublin City archivist; Ms Máire Kennedy, senior librarian, Dublin City Public Libraries; and Ms Ophelia Byrne of the Linen Hall Library, Belfast. The following people have been exceptionally helpful: Mr Brian Coyle; Mr David Donoghue, Irish ambassador to Moscow; Ms Zhenia Studenikina, Moscow; Mr Peter McIvor, first secretary, Irish Embassy, Tokyo; Ms Kazuko Marie Kai, Tokyo; Mr Dennis Behe, Guthrie Theatre, Minneapolis; Mr Ronnie Tallon of Scott Tallon Walker, Architects; Ms Marie Rooney of the Dublin Gate Theatre; An t-Uas. Darach Mac Con Iomaire, Taibhdhearc na Gaillimhe; Mr Richard Mangan of the Raymond Mander and Joe Mitchenson Theatre Collection; Mr Steve MacDonagh of Brandon Book Publishers; the actors Mr Pat Laffan and Mr Frank Kelly (the latter for permission to reproduce cartoons from *Dublin Opinion*); Mr and Mrs Peter Brittain for permission to reproduce cartoons by Miss Grace Plunkett; Ms Heather Kent of the Copthorne Tara Hotel, London, for permission to reproduce their portrait of Sean O'Casey by Robert Ballagh; the designers Ms Bronwen Casson and Ms Wendy Shea; the photographers Ms Amelia Stein and Mr Fergus Bourke; Fr Seán O'Donohoe OFM Cap of *The Capuchin Annual;* Ms Maureen Hurley, who maintains the photographic collection of her father, Mr John J Hurley; and Mr Paul Barry, whose father Mr Dermot Barry was the theatre's principal photographer in the 1960s – three of his superb pictures are reproduced here. A special word of gratitude is appropriate *in memoriam* to the late Ms Tanya Moiseiwitch, whose recollections of the theatre in the 1930s have been so valuable. Most of all, the generous sponsorship of Abhann Productions has made this publication possible.

picture credits

A very large number of illustrations were provided through the Abbey Theatre Archive. Individual photographers represented by the following page numbers are: Dermot Barry 112L, 125, 126. Brandon Book Publishers 161L. Fergus Bourke 33, 38BL, 38BR, 39L, 61–64, 68–70, 71TR, 71BR, 71BL, 87–89, 112R, 120, 128, 129, 131, 132, 138–43, 156-160, 161R, 162, 166, 170, 173. Chancellor Studios, 24, 25. Charles Collins 175. Brian Fitzpatrick 71TL. Keogh Brothers 32R, 45. Tom Lawlor 124, 133, 148BL, 171, 190, 207. Geraint Lewis 193L. Neil Libbert 192. James G Maguire endpapers, 79, 81, 100, 107, 109–11, 123. Paul McCarthy 39R, 189, 194. Kauze Nogakudo 146. Pat Redmond 191. Rex Roberts Studios 50, 54TL, 54TR, 54BR, 54BL. Douglas Robertson 115. John Sarsfield 106, 108. Mike Shaughnessy 86L. Amelia Stein 5, 6, 26, 35, 82, 108, 114, 130, 145, 147, 149–51, 163, 172, 174, 176, 180–88. Illustrations from other sources are: An Clochomhar 86R. An Post 80. *The Capuchin Annual* 60, 78. Dublin City Public Libraries (Bourke Collection) 14R. *Dublin Opinion* 98, 104R. Fáilte Ireland 34 LT, 96, 99T. Hugh Lane Municipal Gallery of Modern Art 55L. John J Hurley 23. Linen Hall Library, Belfast 55R, 65, 66, 83. Ms Tanya Moiseiwitsch 52–53. National Gallery of Ireland 8L, 12TL, 37. National Library of Ireland 12R, 13L, 21, 28, 34BL, 34R, 44BR, 47, 72, 99B. National Photographic Archive 36, 46, 84, 98–99. The National Trust 40. Radio Telefís Eireann 124. Raymond Mander and Joe Mitcheson Collection 32L. Scott Tallon Walker 116. Tyrone Guthrie Centre at Annaghmakerrig 12BL. While every effort has been made to contact all known photographers, some pictures have proved unidentifiable. Any omissions are much regretted, and information leading to identification will be gratefully received and full credits added to any subsequent printings of this book.

Frank McCusker as Nick and Jane Brennan as Deirdre in Bernard Farrell's *The Last Apache Reunion* in 1993.

acknowledgments & picture credits

index